Idon SCENARIO THINKING

How to Navigate the Uncertainties of Unknown Futures

MIRIAM GALT
GARY CHICOINE-PIPER
NELA CHICOINE-PIPER
ANTHONY HODGSON
Foreword by Arie de Geus

Written, Developed and Published by

IDON LTD

EDRADOUR HOUSE PITLOCHRY PERTHSHIRE PH16 5JW SCOTLAND UK
Telephone (UK) 01796 473773 Fax: (UK) 01796 473880

First published in Great Britain 1997

A CIP catalogue record for this book is available from the British Library.

ISBN 0 9530421 0 3

Cover and design by Artworks
Printed by Milne, Tannahill and Methven Ltd, Perth, PH2 0JE

ACKNOWLEDGEMENTS

The authors of this handbook are indebted to a number of people who, over the years of its evolution, have contributed in different ways. Especially we would like to mention the late Julian Romanes who helped with research and drafted the first version of this book. His untimely death was a loss to the team and we know he would be pleased that the enterprise has now come to fruition. Our thanks go also to Frances Heaton-Renshaw whose painstaking reading, critique of clarity, redrafting and general word processing skills have contributed much to the text and layout of this book.

The methods in the book have a track record of application in private and public sector organisations in Europe, America and the Far East. The clients of Idon are all worthy of mention for giving us feedback on the experience of these methods, whether facilitated by Idon or independently used.

We have also been privileged to receive ideas, experienced advice and especially, encouragement from several pioneers in the field of strategy, scenarios and organisational learning. Particularly, our thanks go to Arie de Geus, Kees van der Heijden and Charles Hampden-Turner for their inspiring and mind-stretching influence on us.

The responsibility, however, for the content of this book is down to the authors. We hope the readers and users of the methods will find that practical value can be extracted from our codification of these methods which we offer as a contribution to praxis in the field.

CONTENTS OVERVIEW

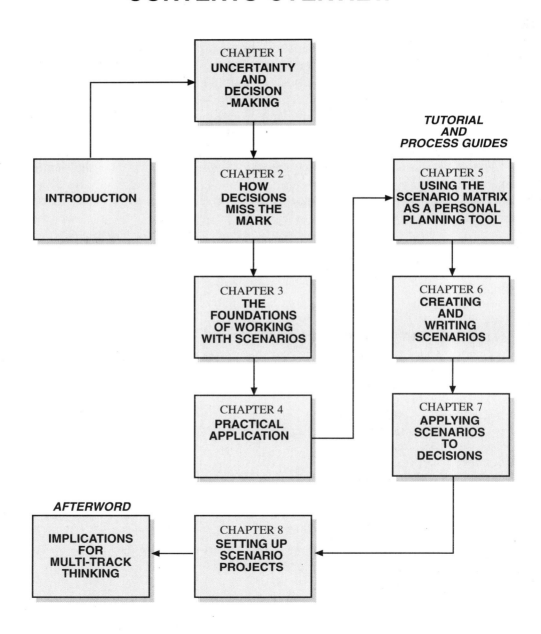

CHAPTER 1
UNCERTAINTY AND DECISION -MAKING

INTRODUCTION

CHAPTER 2
HOW DECISIONS MISS THE MARK

TUTORIAL AND PROCESS GUIDES

CHAPTER 5
USING THE SCENARIO MATRIX AS A PERSONAL PLANNING TOOL

CHAPTER 3
THE FOUNDATIONS OF WORKING WITH SCENARIOS

CHAPTER 6
CREATING AND WRITING SCENARIOS

CHAPTER 4
PRACTICAL APPLICATION

CHAPTER 7
APPLYING SCENARIOS TO DECISIONS

AFTERWORD

IMPLICATIONS FOR MULTI-TRACK THINKING

CHAPTER 8
SETTING UP SCENARIO PROJECTS

CONTENTS

FOREWORD

by Arie de Geus

Change the Language - Change the Reality!

Much of the decision-making in companies has to do with the future. How will the world look? What will the competition do? Will technological developments create surprises?

Most companies deal with the future by trying to reduce the uncertainty of it. They make guesses about what the future will look like by addressing the question: "What will happen....?" And they do so in elaborate corporate processes called "Planning", as well as in their Board and management meetings.

Neurobiology has discovered that the human mind has a much superior way to deal with the future. The brain does not try to reduce the uncertainty of the future by predicting it. The brain deals with the future by constantly asking the question "What will I <u>do</u> when this or that happens.....?" The latter question does not reduce the uncertainty of the future, but it prepares the mind to be ready for action under many possible futures.

The brain is hard-wired for the process of visiting many futures in this action-oriented manner. Board and management meetings work differently. The process of decision-making in companies does not take place between neurons and synapses but between human individuals who meet and talk - i.e. decision-making is language based. "Meeting" is a process of language creation in which the participants in the meeting come to a shared understanding of the meaning of specific words used. In this process of decision-making through meetings and talking, scenarios and hexagons can be a great help.

Scenarios are internally-consistent stories of possible futures - they are the scenery into which the actors walk. The walk is initiated by the meeting addressing the question, "What would we <u>do</u> if this scenario came about?" The many answers to that question become the options that are open to the company under a variety of futures. Those options are expressed by the meeting in words - they create a language for them. Henceforth they can talk about these options in quite precise terms and they will remember the words - they have created a memory

i

of their future! This memory will be extremely useful when the future comes - as it invariably does. The company knows what to look out for and it is better prepared for action.

Talking and creating language in a meeting of corporate individuals is not as easy as it sounds. Many things can go wrong, and do go wrong. People talk but do not listen. Power positions are abused. Emotions take over.

This is where hexagons/idons have a proven track record. They help people calibrate the way they are thinking about the present. They help the group to see relationships and dynamics that are essential to understand the options that are open to them. With attention focused toward the whiteboard, on the idons and not on individual people, thinking is convergent - language becomes concise. Hexagons are powerful tools to help develop the language in which the institutional learning is embodied and which will form the institutional memory. A well-developed memory of the future is a pre-condition for the company to be pro-active rather than reactive - to make its own future rather than submit to it.

Arie de Geus
Author of 'The Living Company'

April 1997

INTRODUCTION

How Scenarios Help Decision-Making

Freedom to Choose

As we exercise our freedom of choice consciously or by default, we incur consequences, experienced as pleasing or painful. Responsibility for our decision-making, manifested through action or inaction, undertaken deliberately or inadvertently, remains ours. Having to make a choice in the face of uncertainty - particularly when the stakes are high - can bring additional pressures to bear that impact on, and often influence, judgement.

So, in the midst of uncertainty, having full confidence to commit to an action, whether as an individual or as part of an organisation, may require the satisfaction of many wide-ranging pre-requisites, including accurate contextual information, some form of traditional forecasting and a feeling of having done 'everything possible' to optimise chances for the desired outcome. The degree to which we attend to these issues is a choice we make.

Limitations of Mindset

Even when motivation to do *"everything possible"* is high, once we start looking more deeply into it we find there are softer issues to take into account that are anything but straight-forward. Arie De Geus, former Head of Planning for the Shell Group puts it well:

"Where you sit and what you've thought determines what you see".

How aware are we of our mindset and the forces driving our opinions and decisions? What are we assuming about our situation and are we questioning those assumptions? How far are we in touch with and deliberately facing the inherent uncertainties that exist? How many possible outcomes do we take into account whilst doing this? What have we not taken into account? Have we considered unexpected events, what might they be? What does our intuition tell us... and... in the light of all this, are we pursuing the right course?

The Dilemma of the Future

Although it could be seen as attractive at times, if offered the power of clairvoyance or prediction as a real option, we are not so sure many of us would indeed choose to have it.

We may be vulnerable in front of an unknown future but seeing the future 'out of context', whether we consider we are prepared for it or not, would bring sudden exposure to experiences of unexpected joys, or, alternatively, unbearable sorrows.

Without preparation - a psychological and emotional understanding of the unfolding of events and time horizons - our feelings of helplessness and disengagement from consequences would be amplified. Foreknowledge of either positive or negative outcomes would undoubtedly alter the conditions of our current existence, even where we are apparently helpless to effect a change.

Should we say it is fortunate then, that we are spared this type of vision, and consequently a confrontation of the difficult dilemma? This might be an over-simplification of the issue. Historically, our desire for knowledge, exploration and understanding of our predicament, wanting control over destiny, does not so easily surrender to complacency.

To what extent are we victims of circumstances, the unexpected, the unknown - and to what extent are we creative participants effecting changes in an unfolding drama? These fundamental questions lie at the core of Scenario Thinking, constituting both its mystery and its challenge. As we enter into dialogue with this issue we are widening our perspectives and increasing our options for exercising more deliberate decision-making toward positive changes.

Scenario Thinking as a Mental Skill
The essence of Scenario Thinking (or Scenario Planning) is *not* about predicting the future and surprisingly enough, *not* about choosing the best way forward, though it is indeed a powerful and invaluable tool which helps this. Its primary value lies in the development of *new faculties* for improved decision-making in those that practise it regularly; faculties that determine *how we are* in the face of the unknown.

Developing these faculties enables us to transcend the specific or localised circumstance solution, to go beyond short-term or one-off successes and acquire a consistency and robustness in coherent long-term decision making. We more rapidly come to know the right questions to ask and where to look for missing pieces to the puzzle; how to spot unique opportunities, choose the best way forward, respond flexibly and quickly in an emergency and so on...with a confident base on which to build.

Without this essential new capability, we may take up Scenario Planning as a discipline but lack the skill and insight to gain its real value.

Contexting Scenarios

Surprisingly, the first step in Scenario thinking - or Multi-Future thinking as we often refer to it at Idon, is to fix ourselves firmly in the present. When thinking about the future, we do so within a context; a starting place or how things are now, gives rise to an opening array of ideas or facts, which in turn are related to some sense of a desired goal or objective.

As we convert this information into well defined 'stories' of possible future situations and what our 'options' for action in them are, we surface the inherent uncertainties facing us that need to be dealt with or overcome. An obvious fact often forgotten, however, is that these uncertainties have sprung out of our original thinking, assumptions, omissions and commissions.

The quality and disposition of original input will strongly influence the flow of thought, handling of material and quality of output. In order to make the best use of scenarios it is important to clarify our intentions and identify the issues or areas to test with the multiple futures. In this book we demonstrate a way of mapping these issues with hexagons which ensures that the widest range of factors is taken into consideration at the outset.

Finally, we hope this publication will enhance your implementation of Scenario Thinking. In the pages that follow we present material for thought along the lines we have been discussing, as well as extensive application guidelines and exercises for thinking in multiple futures. For best practice we recommend you use the material in conjunction with the Idon Scenario Thinking Kits and Idons-For-Thinking™ software.

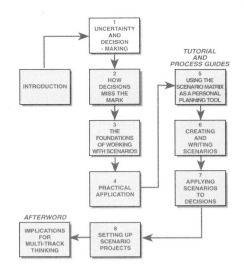

Chapter One

UNCERTAINTY AND DECISION-MAKING

- **Facing Up to Uncertainty**
- **Improving Your Decision-Making**
- **Applying Scenario Thinking**

CHAPTER ONE

UNCERTAINTY AND DECISION-MAKING

Facing Up To Uncertainty

We generally say that things exist in the past, in the present or in the future, but this is too often a simplistic approach, as we discover when engaging in deeper thinking on the subject. Accordingly we often fall into the trap of thinking that there is only one future, failing to include the different possibilities that often come about.

Consider the following three possible futures:

1. The Old Future
This is what is usually called 'The Future'. It is an extrapolation from the past, like a 'what-if' function in a spread sheet. And like a spreadsheet calculation, it is done with a computer of a kind - the human brain. The workings and structure of the human brain often make for linear thinking, which expects a rigid one-story future. Holding several alternatives in mind appears to make each one less probable, instinct being to prefer a definite answer. This preference is sometimes so strong that the brain will often manufacture a prediction with more confidence than substance.

2. The New Future
The new future consists of a set of parallel stories about events in the future. These are called scenarios and none of them has happened yet. When one is thinking of the new future, it is understood that the stories are not certainties, nor are they predictions. They are all possibilities. By considering multiple scenarios, none of which is held as a certainty, one reaches a clarified uncertainty about the future which leads to a more flexible expectation pattern in the brain. This is a fresh perspective, without false certainties.

3. The Real Future
This is what is actually going to happen. No one can say they know this in advance. All one can do is get ready to meet it as it comes. To meet the Real Future with a mental image of the

Old Future is like driving a car into a brick wall. One gets a terrible shock and a sense of having been wholly unprepared for the outcome.

To meet the Real Future with mental images formed by the New Future is to meet it flexibly with some preparation for it, through one or another of the alternative scenarios turning out to be true to some extent. Consequently one is able to respond more efficiently to actual events.

For example, if one were to drive in a car race like the 'Le Mans 24 Hours', the entire team will have taken into account various possibilities and will have considered changes in the weather, so rain tyres for the car will be on hand just in case. If the car's traction needs rain tyres, the pit team will not be caught off guard. At the same time, if the weather clears, they will be quite prepared to go back to dry tyres. The pit team is in a mode of flexibility towards unknown outcomes like the weather. They do not go into shock simply because they do not know the future.

Creating The Multi-Future
If we meet the Real Future with the New Future we have created conditions in which:

1. A correct system of monitoring which future trends appear to be coming into play can be set up with some degree of flexibility and readiness to act.

2. The actual future will be educational in regard to meeting yet further futures down the line.

Failure to face uncertainties with a positive state of mind is Old Future thinking and can be perceived as driving whilst looking in the rear view mirror, living in hope that past successful performances will determine future success.

A notable example of this in the past was the strategic plan for the defence of France with the Maginot Line. This chain of fortifications stretched to the border with Holland and was designed to withstand German attacks of the type experienced in the trench warfare of World War I. When the expected attack came, the German army went around the Maginot Line, by invading Holland (which had remained neutral in the previous war). They also went through the fortifications by using new methods and equipment. The planners of the Maginot line had planned for the previous war.

The way that an organisation develops overall awareness and learning in its membership is through developing mental flexibility in all participants. One of the greatest means of developing this kind of mental flexibility is by exploring alternative realities individually or with others.

If a high enough proportion of individuals in an organisation or department are mentally flexible - aware and learning - then learning can take place. It is therefore important that as many people as possible in that situation participate to some degree in the scenario planning process. If more than 50% have mental flexibility towards the future, then chances are that the organisation or department will show better decision-making with more rapid response of a correct kind to unfolding events.

In analyses of lost opportunities, a common remark is, 'How were we supposed to know? Nobody could have predicted such a situation...' The answer to the question is: 'Through scenario planning there is no need to predict; you only need to consider real possibilities.'

*"Scenario Planning is about making choices **today** with an understanding of how they might turn out ...... Using scenarios is rehearsing the future. You run through the simulated events as if you were already living them. You train yourself to recognise which drama is unfolding. That helps you avoid unpleasant surprises, and know how to act."*

Peter Schwarz - 'The Art of the Long View'

Improving Your Decision-Making

Complexity, Uncertainty and Responsibility

Never before has humanity been challenged with so much knowledge and so much uncertainty. The more we find out, the more uncertain we become about our future and the possible consequences of our choices. At the same time it is important that we make decisions and act with a knowledgeable sense of risk and reward.

Decision-Making as Learning

Most of us do this by 'learning on the job': setting desirable goals, acting so as to achieve them, observing the outcome and making the inevitable necessary corrections. There are good reasons to refine this, both by a process of improvement and by shortening the time taken for the whole cycle. Learning in real time can be slow - the results of some decisions may take years to come in - and the actions taken may be irreversible or costly. As the old saying goes, "Experience is a wonderful teacher but the bills she sends in are terrific."

Learning - understanding the meaning of events and applying that understanding cross-functionally - is central in our lives. Each of us constantly weaves patterns of meaning out of our experience, in which places, people, actions and events are significant because of the way they are related, the way they fit into a story. This unconscious process tends to filter out and discard anything which we find meaningless and leaves the rest arranged into a plot or sequence. This explaining and understanding procedure underpins all thinking, simple and complex. For example, in looking back over the kind of day we have had, we will arrange things into patterns of cause and effect: "I went to the meeting after lunch and the new presentation was a big success; all the preparation time really paid off". A similar narrative approach is used when we look forward into the future: "The department re-organisation will have to begin with a briefing meeting for key people or there will be confusion and wasted effort."

This is what we all use when we rehearse outcomes in our minds. Sometimes it is called visualisation, or story building. After first filtering our experiences we then imagine various possibilities which might occur and consider results which differ from our plans.

Learning From the Future

Just as our memories of people and circumstances in our past shape and affect our behaviour through a combination of mood, attitude and expectations based on previous experiences, so too our 'memories of the future' - or mental rehearsals - also affect our behaviour. Cognitive research has shown that perception is affected by expectation and thinking is influenced by associations. We tend to see what we are looking for and to hear what we want. In one study of self-fulfilling prophecies, a group of primary school teachers were told that some of the pupils in their incoming classes had been shown in tests to be highly intelligent, whereas the other children in the classes were of normal intelligence.

In fact this was untrue; all the pupils in the classes were within a statistically normal band of intelligence. Nonetheless, the 'intelligent' pupils soon out-performed their classmates not merely on graded tests but across a range of other performance measures. It seems that the teachers' expectations of these children's performances helped to shape the actual performance. If our expectations can shape the future actions and achievements of another, how much more effect must they have upon our own actions?

Rehearsing Multiple Outcomes

Our visualisations or stories of the future will definitely steer us towards making that type of future real. This means that we should be taking great care in our thinking when constructing images of the future. Since these memories of the future give us a degree of creative choice about outcomes, it is worth investing time and attention towards improving the odds of getting what we want.

Having said this however, improving the odds does not guarantee total control. As we frequently experience, the future holds surprises and unforeseen challenges. Managing change is about responding successfully to this.

When we admit uncertainty, we are not fixed in anticipation of what we believe will happen, we are taking the first step toward accelerating our capacity to learn. If the future is unknown we are free to entertain and explore different futures. When we visualise several different possibilities and ask ourselves how we would act in each set of circumstances, we are rehearsing the outcomes we would want in each case and preparing memories of the future as pathways of probability.

"Often managers prefer the illusion of certainty to understanding risks and realities. If the forecaster fails in his task, how can the manager be blamed? But in the long run, this denial of uncertainty sets the stage for surprises, shattering the manager's confidence in his or her ability to look ahead. Scenarios allow a manager to say, "I am prepared for whatever happens". **It is this ability to act with a knowledgeable sense of risk and reward that separates both the business executive and the wise individual from a bureaucrat or a gambler."**

Peter Schwarz - 'The Art of the Long View'

If the future is not in fact like any of the alternatives we anticipated, there is still a benefit. We have grown away from our old expectation of one specific future and we have embraced the uncertainty of multiple futures. We are more able to accept whatever comes and quicker to understand what it means to us and our business. This makes our response time shorter, so our learning will quicken.

The real pay-off of scenario thinking is not future prediction but better change management. Describing how Shell adopted scenario thinking ahead of the major oil price shocks in the early 1980's (and reaped the benefits accordingly), Pierre Wack, former Head of the Business Environment Division of Royal Dutch/Shell Group Planning, comments that "forecasts are usually constructed on the assumption that tomorrow's world will be much like today's. But sooner or later forecasts will fail when they are needed most: in anticipating major shifts in the business environment that make whole strategies obsolete."

Business trends reveal that successful organisations present some similar characteristics relative to survival, synergy and anticipation:

Past: *Survival*	**Present:** *Synergy*	**Future:** *Anticipation*
Research shows that the survival of an organisation is related to its capacity to learn and adapt within a changing business environment	Successful organisations respond coherently and effectively in the midst of change Organisational effectiveness is determined by the degree and quality of continuous personal and group learning	Accelerating change driven by innovation shortens the future planning time horizon requiring a sound but creative approach to strategy and implementation

In a 1983 Royal Dutch Shell Survey it was revealed that: "One third of the firms in the Fortune 500 in 1970 had vanished"
(de Geus, 1988)

In other words, when our assumptions become outdated, we must learn afresh. Knowing that the mind uses assumptions as the building blocks for thinking, and that this process goes on below the level of consciousness, gives us a new interest in exploring and understanding the mental models underlying the stories of the future which we continually create.

"External scenarios are derived from shared and agreed upon mental models of the external world. They are created as internally consistent and challenging descriptions of possible futures. They are intended to be representative of the ranges of possible future developments and outcomes in the external world. What happens in them is essentially outside our control...... Herman Kahn saw as the great value of the scenario approach that it allowed the observer to engage in value-free exploration. It allows executives to see the world through different lenses, stretching beyond their conventional mental map. Value-free scenarios can help them see things they were not looking for."

Kees van der Heijden - 'Scenarios - The Art of Strategic Conversation'

Scenarios as Mental Models

Pierre Wack and his successors at Shell focused on improving the mental models used by the operational managers in making decisions. A good mental map of the manager's decision territory will include a well developed ability to distinguish signal from noise - good pattern recognition. Where this is less developed, a manager will be less prepared for change management. He or she will be more dependent on operating with existing patterns. New signals may be discounted as low in meaning and precious time will go by before the manager learns to take new factors into account.

Effectively this process is taking learning by experience in the present and placing it up ahead in the future. Nothing can ever substitute completely for experience but airlines know that the training of pilots in flight simulators has advantages over the exclusive use of real aircraft. This kind of 'virtual experience' can supply new freedom to discover, shorten learning loops, reduce the penalties of failure - without negating feedback - and develop more flexible mental models.

For the value of that, Arie de Geus, former Head of Group Planning for Shell, remarks: "Outcomes depend on the ability of managers to absorb what is going on in the business environment and to act on that information with appropriate business moves. In other words, they depend on learning. We think of planning as learning. We understand that the only competitive advantage the company of the future will have is its managers' ability to learn faster than their competitors. So the companies that succeed will be those that continually nudge their managers towards revising their views of the world."

A sustained learning approach securing competitive leadership requires:

- an accelerated pace of learning to outwit uncertainties, new developments and changes in the business environment

- practical utilisation of knowledge and skills in new supportive development techniques and technologies

- the pursuit of widening horizons through environmental scanning, scenario planning and probing for organisational drivers

The outcome for the corporate strategic thinking process is not merely new models of reality within managers' minds. More important than any specific change is a new willingness to consider alternatives and to include uncertainty in the decision process as a natural component. The managers' decisions will be better focused and less bounded by assumptions. Uncertainty, then, will not be feared but embraced as a challenge, a source for creative potential and competitive edge.

Blind Spots

There is more at stake here than learning flexibility and improving our capacity for change management and more even than improving our 'signal to noise ratio'. Scenario thinking can directly improve the quality of decision-making by focusing attention on how we perceive, classify and use information. In our natural decision-making strategies we all use a small number of heuristics - rules of thumb - which look only at the parts of a problem which are most likely to reach a correct solution. These are well adapted for success but become a liability when they are applied outside their range. The quality of decision-making depends, among other things, upon the recognition of these so as to avoid human errors.

Applying Scenario Thinking

We have identified three types of application of scenario thinking. The most common so far is in an organisational context where executive and planning teams use scenarios to help generate, clarify and test strategies. The next application is that of a team involved in a project that has a high level of uncertainty, where it is essential to find a common approach to managing that uncertainty. The third application is at the individual level, where a person faces a choice or a change which has uncertainties out of his/her direct control, yet he/she must take a decision to move forward. Let us look at these three applications more closely.

Individual Application

The individual brain is the starting point for all multi-future thinking. Teams and organisations cannot begin to apply it without skilled individuals. What this book sets out to do at this level is provide a step by step guide to framing and taking a decision in the face of personal uncertainties. This method concentrates on the scenario matrix as the main tool. This is distinct from the usual cross-impact matrix. We call it a *generative matrix*. The purpose is to generate new options and ideas in answer to the question, "What if I pursue this decision in this future? What then?"

Although this way of thinking may be unfamiliar as a conscious practice, the essence of the process is natural to the structure of the human brain. There is a part of the brain dedicated to "memory of the future" which is constantly and subconsciously rehearsing "what if?" By practising the methods in this book this latent capacity is developed into a useful skill.

Team Application

Very often we need to share our decisions with others - partner, family or work group. This is where an explicit visual method becomes helpful in a different way. It provides a framework within which people can share their concerns about the future, develop a shared perspective and create more flexible options to deal with that future. In this sense using the scenario method is a shared learning process. The scenarios provide a playground in which we can "step out of the box" and have more chance of changing our mindset. This is important to avoid being stuck in a tunnel vision which will cause our decisions to "miss their mark".

Organisation Application

The place of scenario thinking at the organisational level takes things a stage further. A team may be temporary but an organisation, especially a living company, strives for continued evolution and adaptation to changing circumstances beyond the life-time of any one team. Traditional planning has been based on an approach that can be called *Rationalistic*. Objectives are set, plans are made, choices are taken which are then passed on for implementation. This rational approach largely depends on a single set of assumptions and a forecast of a single future. Grafting scenarios onto a rational approach misses a number of important things essential to their effectiveness.

The lessons of complexity science show us that it is not possible to specify in advance the attributes of such a system. Clearly the world at large is very complex. The world, as time passes, reveals emergent properties that inherently can never be anticipated; in such a world the rational approach increasingly fails us. An alternative approach is the *Processual* which accepts at the start that any decision is simply a temporary step on a journey through time and that the context in which those decisions are being made will inevitably change in ways that cannot be predicted. Scenario thinking is one type of intelligent process that can deal with this challenge adaptively.

To apply scenarios in this way requires that we do not treat a scenario exercise as a "one off" from which to make the "grand strategic choice". Scenarios need to be treated much more as a decision background evolving over time. Scenarios themselves need revision, evolution and even radical reframing. To use an analogy from the physics of radioactivity, they have a relatively short half-life. The processual approach is a new paradigm for choosing within a flow of decisions rather than treating decisions as widely separated and isolated events.

In this book we use the term *decision intent* to stand for the general direction we intend to pursue. This intent sustains over time the flow of decisions. We use the term *decision options* to describe those more specific actions we might take, depending on our choice. In an uncertain world with emergent properties, we need ways of enriching our store of options so that as we reach points of choice in the flow of events we can stay "on the mark" of our direction. The next section is called "How decisions miss the mark" as an expression of this concept.

The challenge, we shall see, is that how we frame our decisions can be trapped in tunnel vision. This means the range of options we will think of or entertain is restricted. Since the real future will have features outside of our tunnel vision, we get knocked off course. Multi-future thinking acts as a great stimulus to enlarge the space within which we generate options, thus empowering our choices as we follow our intent.

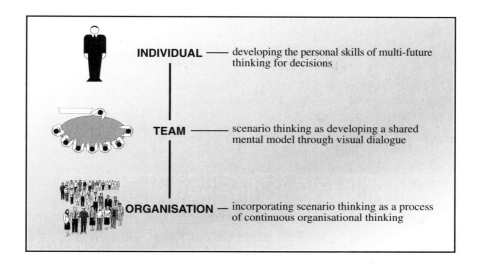

INDIVIDUAL —— developing the personal skills of multi-future thinking for decisions

TEAM —— scenario thinking as developing a shared mental model through visual dialogue

ORGANISATION — incorporating scenario thinking as a process of continuous organisational thinking

Scenarios then, in an organisation, should be incorporated as part of a strategic learning spiral. They are probably one of the most powerful ways, together with systems thinking and issue mapping, for enabling organisational learning. They help people to create a common language with which to interpret the changing scenery of the future as it unfolds and the impact this has on their enterprise.

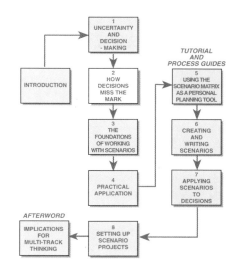

Chapter Two

HOW DECISIONS MISS THE MARK

- **The Idea of the First Causal Heuristic**
- **The Five Common Errors in Decision-Making**
- **Framing Decisions**

"The mind can only see what it is prepared to see. This is now widely accepted. That is why there is such a need for hypotheses, speculation and provocation when examining data. Without such new 'frameworks' we would only be able to see the data in the old way."

Edward de Bono - 'Water Logic'

CHAPTER TWO

HOW DECISIONS MISS THE MARK

The Idea of the First Causal Heuristic

We often construct causal scenarios: stories in which one event causes another, leading from the original situation to the outcome. If it is easy for us to envisage a plot producing the result we want, we believe that the outcome is probable. If it is hard to put together the mental story successfully, we believe that the outcome is correspondingly unlikely. We judge the probability of achieving a particular goal by the ease with which a mental simulation reaches that goal. So, the ease with which examples or events come to mind is an important determinant in decision-making.

A young man contemplating his future can easily visualise taking a job in a local company, perhaps in construction. Perhaps he has seen work sites in the area. He may have watched the progress of the buildings under construction and he may know or be acquainted with workers employed by the company. This will all contribute to help him think that work for such a company is a probable future for him, since he will be able to visualise himself at similar work sites, mixing and conversing with the other employees and acting out roles he has seen at different work sites.

He may be more ambitious and wonder about life as a doctor. If he can visualise the steps along the way - acceptance at medical school, long hours of study, success in competitive exams and life as a junior doctor in a teaching hospital - then this outcome too could be considered probable.

It is harder to imagine the stages along the route to becoming President of the United States - there is too little information and it is too hard to make a meaningful story of it. Something as unthinkable as this automatically becomes dismissed as highly improbable.

Most of us will have noticed the first causal scenario heuristic at work in our own thinking, in something like the following example. Consider two travellers, Michael and Ruth, both scheduled to leave the airport on different flights but at the same time. The two travelled from town in the same car, were caught in a traffic jam and arrived at the airport thirty minutes after the scheduled departure time of their flights. Michael is told that his flight left on time. Ruth is told that her flight was delayed and just left five minutes ago. Who do you suppose is more upset?

In research, 96% of all those questioned said that Ruth would be more upset. Why should this be, since both had the same outcome? The reasoning is that both Michael and Ruth will engage in a reconstruction of events on the way to the airport in order to test how close they came to making their flight. It is easier to see how Ruth could have saved five minutes in her reconstruction, say by not buying a newspaper or having the traffic jam ease slightly. It is harder to see how Michael could make a story saving thirty minutes. So most people project their own causal scenario heuristic onto our two fictional travellers and sympathise more with Ruth.

It must be emphasised that the ease with which things come to mind has nothing to do with probability. If we find it easy to imagine our new product quickly gaining market share, or easy to foresee continuing increases in share prices, it does not follow that these things will happen. In the same way, to find something hard to imagine does not make it improbable. Here are a couple of other examples of the first causal scenario heuristic at work:

> "A severe depression like that of 1920-21 is outside the range of probability."
> Harvard Economic Society - Weekly Letter November 16 1929.

> "Heavier than air flying machines are impossible" Lord Kelvin - British mathematician, physicist and president of the British Royal Society, c 1895.

Cognitive Causes of Over-Confidence

* What is out of sight is out of mind
 - we fail to envision unusual events and tune out unacceptable futures

* Anchoring
 - best guesses dominate our calibration, prejudicing our range of confidence

* The Confirmation Bias
 - leaning towards one perspective, we select only confirming evidence

* Hindsight
 - believing the world is more predictable than it is, we harbour illusions of omniscience

---

The first causal scenario is not only common to us all but is boosted and maintained by other heuristics.

The Five Common Errors In Decision-Making

The Anchoring Error

Anchoring means that when we must guess or estimate a probability we are influenced by whatever figure is supplied from within the situation, whether or not this is relevant or even rational. We anchor our estimate close to some base. In one research study, participants were asked to estimate the number of African countries in the United Nations. First though, the experimenters spun a roulette wheel, which selected a random number between 0 and 100. The participants were asked to say whether the answer to the question was higher or lower than the selected number and then to give their estimate. The roulette wheel's number acted as an anchor for the estimates. If the wheel stopped at 10, people would estimate 25 as the number of African countries in the United Nations. If the wheel stopped at 65, people estimated 45.

In an even more dramatic demonstration of anchoring, students were asked to estimate the year of the defeat in Europe of Attila the Hun and asked to say whether it was before or after a figure based on the last three digits of their own telephone number. This figure visibly influenced the estimates.

Random anchors therefore can change people's opinions as much as rational ones. This process supports the first causal scenario heuristic, because in practice we will anchor our estimates and opinions close to what we can imagine, rather than according to what may in fact be probable.

The Adjustment Error

This makes us reluctant to change our minds once we have formed an opinion, which in turn often leads to resistance to new information or alternative modes of reasoning. History is full of examples of this, from the resistance within the medical profession to the use of antiseptics, to the reluctance of First World War generals to adapt tactics to suit barbed wire and the machine gun. Closer to home, we can probably all recall occasions when we persist in looking for a lost object in a place we have already searched thoroughly, because we are unable to give up the belief that it must be there. This heuristic particularly reinforces the first causal scenario heuristic because it inhibits us from considering other possibilities already within our experience.

The Entrapment Error

This encourages deeper and deeper investment into an unsatisfactory decision, because of the need to make good on the previous investment. Anybody who has spent money on fixing up a car is likely to be aware of this heuristic as soon as the car needs further repairs; it goes against the grain not to keep fixing it up. Historians have argued that the United States government fell prey to this heuristic in prosecuting the Vietnam War; too much had been invested to allow a withdrawal even after it became clear the war was not winnable. The well known dollar bill auction also illustrates entrapment.

One person announces to a group that he will auction a one dollar bill to the highest bidder. A rule of the auction is that at the end of the auction the second highest bidder must also pay the amount he or she bid but will receive nothing in return. Played with these rules, bids on the single dollar have occasionally reached as high as twenty dollars because nobody wanted to be a losing bidder.

In business, this heuristic is particularly evident when considering new investments. For example, one steel company discovered that hundreds of thousands of dollars could be saved by replacing hot-metal mixing technology with direct-pouring technology. But there was considerable resistance to this because senior engineers complained that the analysis did not include the cost of the hot metal mixers which had been purchased for $3 million a few years earlier.

Entrapment is deeply intertwined with the first causal scenario heuristic. It is clearly easier to envisage a previous unsuccessful investment turning out right next time, than to consider other unknown possibilities. And on the other hand, the more a particular pattern of behaviour is repeated, the more we will believe that success is probable... Here we can see a deep seated and common confusion between probability and repetition. If the odds of a spun coin landing heads up are even and it lands tails up ten times in a row, what are the odds of another tails? The odds are still fifty fifty. The coin has no memory of its previous run of tails. Repetition of the event does not alter the odds.

AFTER FIFTEEN ROLLS, THE NEXT ONE HAS GOT TO BE A SIX!

The Yardstick Error

This is all a question of what you will use to measure by. In one survey, managers were posed two decision situations. In the first they were asked to imagine they were in a shop about to buy a new watch for £70. A friend enters and says he has seen an identical watch in another shop two streets away, for £40. There is no difference in service between the shops. Would they travel the two streets to save £30?

About 90% of the managers said they would.

Then they were asked to imagine themselves in a shop about to buy a new video camera for £800. A friend enters and says there is an identical camera two streets away for £770. There is no difference in service between the two shops. Would they travel the two streets to save the £30?

In this situation only about 50% of the managers would make the extra effort, although the saving is the same in both situations.

The Over-Confidence Error

This has three separate parts within it. Firstly, people resist looking for examples which will prove them wrong, instead seeking examples and information which will prove them right. Secondly, we are poor at setting a margin of error for decisions. Thirdly, the hindsight factor will operate to reduce learning from previous errors and boost perceptions of accuracy of predictions even when this is not the case.

Researchers at the Wharton Applied Research Centre examined dozens of companies' strategy-formulation processes and repeatedly found planners using computer information systems simply to produce data supporting the strategies they had already decided to adopt. For personal insight into this heuristic, ask yourself how often you ask 'disconfirming questions' - questions designed to disprove something you believe. For example, suppose a manager is quite confident that his or her product's quality is superior to the competition. Everything, from consumer research through feedback from distributors, up to in-house product tests, says so. Has he or she ever asked a question of consumers such as, "What makes you think Brand X's quality is higher than our brand's quality?" The odds are not. This question could only bring bad news and is therefore unnecessary.

We all tend to be too confident about things we know little of. What is curious is that research shows that we also tend to be too confident even in our areas of expertise. For example, when managers in the chemicals industry were given questions specific to their own company and industry, they exhibited striking over-confidence. They were asked to give answers in which they were ninety percent confident, so that they should have been wrong only ten per cent of the time. However the actual answers were wrong fifty percent of the time. Even when asked to give answers with only a fifty percent confidence range, the managers could not do it.

The hindsight error is fairly well known and can be seen in action if you turn back to our examples of the first causal scenario heuristic. Both Lord Kelvin and the authors of the Harvard Economic Society's Weekly Letter may seem foolish to us, because of our exaggeration of what they could have anticipated.

In general the over-confidence heuristic not only operates as a self-perpetuating error because it prevents us from registering properly where our errors really lay but it also fully supports the first causal scenario heuristic because we accept evidence which confirms that our view of the probable future really is happening and we tune out evidence to the contrary.

Framing Decisions

As Edward Russo and Paul Schoemaker* have pointed out, how a decision is framed has a great deal to do with the outcome. This can be illustrated by a thought experiment. Imagine that you have decided to see a play and paid the admission price of £20. As you enter the theatre, you find you have lost the ticket. The seat was not marked and the ticket is not recoverable. Would you pay another £20 for another ticket?

Now imagine that you have decided to see a play where the admission price is £20. As you enter the theatre you find you have lost £20. Would you still pay £20 for the ticket?

Most people would answer "yes" to the second case but feel some reluctance in the first case, because they see the situation as equivalent to paying £40 for the ticket. Here the only variable is the decision frame.

Framing can focus attention on possible gains or on possible losses. People tend to avoid risks when they think that they are dealing with gains and tend to take risks when they think that they are dealing with losses. For instance, people asked to decide on different strategies of how to catch and save the most bottles falling off a wall, will choose a riskier strategy when

*see Bibliography

the bottles are described as half empty, than when the bottles are described as half full. Doctors offered the chance to prescribe new treatments for patients do so markedly less often when the risk is framed as "10% will die" than when it is framed as "90% will survive". The frame or description affects the amount of risk you are prepared to take. The decision frame heuristic is a strong one (i.e. there is a pronounced shift in perceptions), it is common among all types of people and it still happens even when you are aware of it.

Much of Shell's work with scenarios has grown out of the requirement to realign managers' decision frames or mental models, to allow for better decision-making.

So as decision-makers we can become aware that our decision-making process rests upon views of the future which:

•   are judged plausible or implausible only according to our ability to imagine them
•   if based upon estimates, are strongly influenced by any associated input, such as suggestions or forecasts, regardless of their origin or validity
•   are much less accurate than we believe
•   are shaped by the circumstances in which they were first conceived
•   we are reluctant to adjust even when we have evidence that they are misaligned
•   we are ever more motivated to support once we have acted on them
•   tend to act as self fulfilling prophecies.

Scenarios as Antidotes
Scenario thinking helps us to counterbalance these in-built heuristics and achieve more effective results. This kind of discipline is vital because simply knowing about biases does not prevent them. By contexting our decision areas in several scenarios we make ourselves view the decision in several frames. This challenges any bias our in-built heuristics may be giving us.

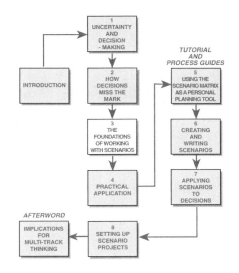

Chapter Three

THE FOUNDATIONS OF WORKING WITH SCENARIOS

- **How Scenario Thinking Works**
- **Limits to Conventional Planning**
- **Decision-Making as Learning**
- **Constructing Multiple Futures**
- **Decision Thinking With Scenarios**
- **Decision Robustness and Resilience**
- **Environmental Sensitivity**
- **Structural Principles of Scenarios**
- **Overview of Scenario Construction**

CHAPTER THREE

THE FOUNDATIONS OF
WORKING WITH SCENARIOS

How Scenario Thinking Works

Scenarios - Exercise Playgrounds for the Mind

In thinking about the future, people seem to relate best to concrete narratives which are consistent and coherent. In other words, we need complete stories which describe and make real as far as possible a world which is different from the present and which is challenging to our thinking. These are scenarios: exercise courts for the mind, where heuristics get aired and decision processes are thoroughly coached, developed and tested for robustness.

Scenario Planning

Scenario planning can be seen as two distinct processes: scenario generation and scenario thinking, with separate starting points involving distinct methods and with different goals. They are often, but not necessarily, undertaken by different teams in an organisation. For example, the planners will develop scenarios and executives are challenged to think with them.

Scenario Generation

Scenario generation is the process of developing and fleshing out two or more stories which produce a few alternative and internally consistent pathways into the future. These acknowledge uncertainty and aim at structuring and understanding it, but not merely by criss-crossing variables and producing multiple outcomes. The point is to have a set of stories that illuminate the major forces driving the system, their interrelationships and the critical uncertainties.

The developed stories may be supported by a great deal of fine detail projected from research and from expert opinions and may reach a high level of narrative sophistication. Ideally they will blend fact - in the sense of highly-probable trends and near-unavoidable events - with fiction, in the sense of creative leaps and discontinuities in present assumptions. If a scenario

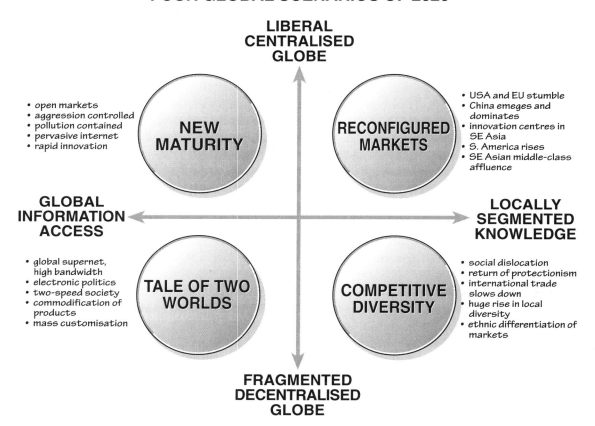

FOUR GLOBAL SCENARIOS OF 2020

LIBERAL CENTRALISED GLOBE

GLOBAL INFORMATION ACCESS

LOCALLY SEGMENTED KNOWLEDGE

FRAGMENTED DECENTRALISED GLOBE

NEW MATURITY

- open markets
- aggression controlled
- pollution contained
- pervasive internet
- rapid innovation

RECONFIGURED MARKETS

- USA and EU stumble
- China emeges and dominates
- innovation centres in SE Asia
- S. America rises
- SE Asian middle-class affluence

TALE OF TWO WORLDS

- global supernet, high bandwidth
- electronic politics
- two-speed society
- commodification of products
- mass customisation

COMPETITIVE DIVERSITY

- social dislocation
- return of protectionism
- international trade slows down
- huge rise in local diversity
- ethnic differentiation of markets

is not disconcerting and challenging, it is probably not worthwhile. The same is true if it is not plausible to people with experience in that domain or line of business.

Scenario Thinking

This involves executives and other decision-makers using previously-generated scenarios as thinking and learning tools. The process involves temporarily adopting the variables of one story and extending these by imagination and discussion to produce a coherent shared perspective on decision contexts and key information. Then the participants must work together to simulate key decisions within the parameters of the given story.

Such decisions should be rationalised and justified in the light of the scenario story and the organisation's overall strategic direction or intent. This kind of 'what-if' questioning takes mutual support and must be extensive in order to clarify what the best decision would be and to illuminate the underlying assumptions. The fluid quality of working with a highly detailed, relevant, consistent but imaginary story, helps participants to flush out and recognise the workings of their own decision heuristics.

By working through this process with more than one scenario, managers can also recognise and become familiar with the decision frames projected into each of the scenario worlds. By searching for a decision option which is viable in each decision frame, they can derive a robust decision option for implementation in the present.

This process of deriving robust options from examining alternative worlds, if repeatedly iterated, will enable a cybernetic approach towards decision-making and problem solving and will quite rapidly evolve an emergent strategic direction which will be independent of the outcome of any particular story world.

By the application of this discipline, we can move from reactive thinking to proactive thinking and develop a strategy during decision-making which will stand up under pressure from the unknown.

Limits to Conventional Planning

"Planning is about the tension between an organisation and its outside world. It uses processes to bring the system back into harmony."
       Arie De Geus - 'Planning as Learning', extract from Harvard Business Review, 1988

Strategy for an organisation is about the way the leaders of that organisation reconcile its mission with the environment in which they find themselves. This environment includes all the kinds of dimensions that need to be taken into account - technical, social, political and ecological - and it also includes the future, since missions have to be carried out over long periods of time.

Dimensions to Consider

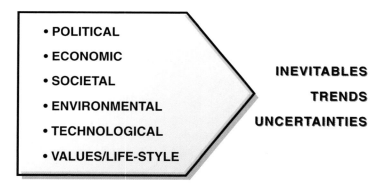

The tendency in plans is to assume that this wider environment is predictable. Based on forecasts, strategy is frozen into budgets, plans and structures.

The plan then assumes a future that validates the plan and this view of the future dominates our decision-making: it is the future we bet on without any way of guaranteeing it will come to pass. We call this the "old future" or the default scenario. It is usually based on some form of extrapolation or forecasting. It is also based on our mindset.

Mindset is the pattern of projected perception we lay on the outside world and sustain through our belief system; this pattern is very hard to change. Our mindset tends to hold us to a default scenario.

```
MINDSET BARRIERS TO HUMAN EFFECTIVENESS

    1. Limited conscious working memory
    2. Poor prospective memory
    3. Bias to see what we expect
    4. Mental models trapped in sequence of information
    5. Naturally slow to renew mental models
    6. Limited bandwidth for information and ideas
    7. Motivation can block openness
    8. Group dynamics causes "groupthink"
    9. Single brain has space/time limitation
```

This is fine where these forecasts hold but we live in a world increasingly shaken by discontinuities and sudden changes. Uncertainty plagues the future so that our plans do not hold up to the stream of real events.

Decision-Making as Learning

In a fluid and changing environment, applying default scenarios leads us into shocks and surprises. Flexible strategies must be developed that go beyond the fixed five-year plan to a vision of the way ahead that is capable of being modified at every twist and turn of events, whilst allowing progress toward the goal. In a fluid environment there are many possible futures and in entertaining them, strategy must embrace the "what if" questions that go outside the reach of our habitual mindset. It is somewhat like the weather. It may be fine; it may rain; what if it snows? Each "what if" question requires a different story of the future; a scenario. Each story will be equally plausible if we can entertain its assumptions. All stories will challenge the assumptions upon which our default scenario is based. Scenarios are distinctly structured views of the future that are self consistent and plausible.

Setting Up the "What if?" Thinking

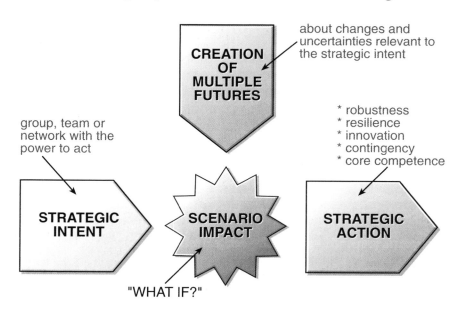

> **STRATEGY AND SCENARIOS NEED WORKING ON TOGETHER**
>
> - the value of scenarios will be better realised if they are used to test current strategic intent
> - strategic intent is more than the most recent business plan
> - it requires a process of strategic conversation to surface and exchange current concerns about the direction and future of the organisation
> - the key is the generative cross impact between strategic intent and several different images of the future

Each distinct future is something from which we can learn how to reconcile our mission with the environment. In the face of the unknown there cannot be pre-determined answers. Thus, strategy ceases to be a fixed plan but rather a learning process that leads to continuous improvement in the alignment of the organisation to its environment.

The Idon Scenario Method

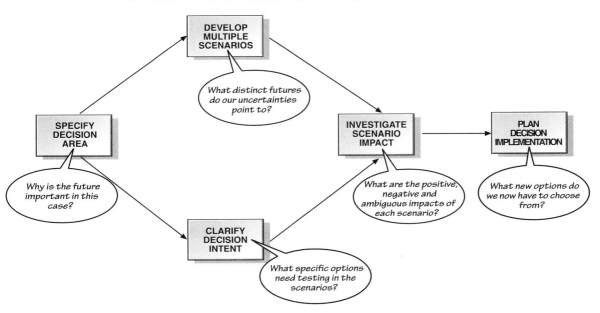

Constructing Multiple Futures

To construct scenarios we need a process that helps us to escape our dominant mindset. A wide variety of perspectives needs to be gathered from outside the confines of the organisation culture as well as from within it. From these perspectives, imagination and logic must be combined to write stories of the future. These stories not only portray images of the future but also a pathway of events through time that could lead us from where we are now to that future world. Underlying this must be an understanding of the driving forces that are likely to be shaping the future. Crucial to the chance that different futures might arise is the idea of "knife-edge criticality", the very small events that trigger vast changes. These are like the switches that route us to one future rather than another. Underlying all this are certain deep structures of forces that determine varieties of behaviour. These structures can be modelled with systems thinking to help us see how different outcomes might emerge.

CREATING GOOD SCENARIOS

- a rich variety of perspectives
- openness to entertain possibilities outside the current belief system
- coverage of crucial dimensions: technical, economic, political, social, environmental etc.
- appreciation of deeper dynamic structures behind alternative scenarios
- identification of pathways to different futures and turning points where the direction shifts
- embedding of future scenarios in the present to activate environmental scanning

---

SOME TYPICAL ERRORS IN USING SCENARIOS

- confusion of scenarios with predictions or forecasts
- scenarios too simplistically differentiated ("golden age" versus "doomsday")
- too narrow in scope and hence still "in the box"
- not focused on areas of significant impact
- poor process (if any) for engaging executive teams in shared strategic thinking
- poor balance of logic and imagination

Decision Thinking With Scenarios

When we have created several scenarios, we use these to improve our decision thinking. Firstly we have to convert our mission or intent into several parallel concerns. These might be policy options, they might be strategies, or they might be changes we believe are necessary. Essentially they are a set of concerns about outcome where we experience the pressure of uncertainty.

These intentions or options then need to be tested out in each future as if we were enacting them in that world. This generates new thinking which is stimulated by the factors in that future and the way these challenge our normal assumptions. The new thinking may be about how to make our strategy robust or "future-proof". On the other hand they may stimulate us to invent more options and expand our flexibility. They may also identify crucial new learning themes in areas where we have not previously placed attention and resources. This cross impact can be represented as a generative matrix.

The Scenario Impact Matrix

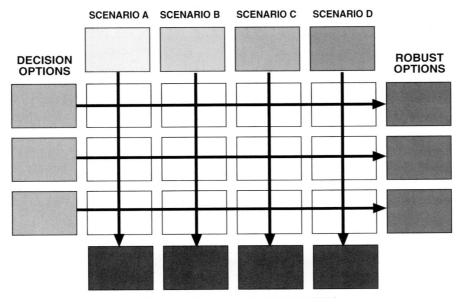

THE IMPACT OF SCENARIOS ON DECISION-MAKING

How Resilient? • actions we should be doing anyway but we overlooked • actions we should take until unfolding events show we should drop them • actions we need to have ready for a specific future • actions to influence the future positively or negatively	**How Competent?** • robust core skills essential for all futures • capabilities needed to give advantage in the longer term • core knowledge and skills to be successful in a specific future • lateral leap competencies we need but have no basis for at present

These new views will also help alert us to developments in the present that are pointing to particular futures that we would otherwise have missed. We do not pick up information from the environment in areas where we have not previously entertained its relevance.

Decision Robustness and Resilience

Being able to cope with contingencies also gives us a sense of power and confidence. If we think about alternative options and we are considering different possible futures, no one of which we are sure is the one that is going to happen, then we would obviously prefer to take a decision which could lead to success whatever the future holds. This would be a robust decision. An attractive strategy might give a high pay off in Scenario A but it would fail in Scenario B. That is not robust if we attribute significant weight to the possibility that Scenario B could occur. However we may need an option prepared for just one future scenario in case things turn out to go that way.

Environmental Sensitivity

Supposing our time horizon for thinking about the future of our business is ten to fifteen years? One might ask, "If the future is so uncertain, isn't writing scenarios now little different from science fiction?". It becomes clear that this is not the case if we understand the link between developing scenarios of the future and a deeper understanding of what is going on right now in the present.

Any interpretation a group of people may give about the world is conditioned by the patterns of perception in each member of the group which have been acquired through a limited life experience. Diverse experts, for example, see quite different things going on and value them quite dissimilarly. To build robust scenarios, we need to take as wide a range of perceptions as possible into our thinking. These impressions hold valuable keys to current and future trends.

There are always pockets of the future in the present. Some countries do things today that will take five or ten years to reach other countries. Some sectors of society are right now living in a way that is our future. Some people have ideas that will take twenty years to incubate and become generally accepted. Technologies exist that people have not yet heard of that will one day be commonplace. By looking around us and seeing what is happening we can pick up vital clues about how the future may already be coming about.

A pre-condition of developing a scenario approach then, is to set up better ways of getting to know what is going on now as seen through a range of different eyes. One way this is done is to gain access to and interview a diverse range of people who have special perceptions about what is happening. Each of these will offer a fresh perspective to enrich our picture and keep us from falling into the default scenario.

A further benefit of scenario thinking is that, having been through a scenario exercise, we become more alert to the weak signals coming in from the environment that might give us early warning or indication of unfolding or adapting trends.

Structural Principles of Scenarios

By scanning the environment in this way we can begin to uncover layers in what is going on. There are dominant features that look as if they are going to persist under any future scenario. These we call inevitables - for example, certain population statistics - a metaphor here might be rocks in the sea bed. Another aspect we call driving forces. These can be likened to the major currents under the sea. An example would be increasing global competition. A further layer is current trends. These are like the surface currents that may increase or decrease in different cycle times. An example would be the trend of increasing and decreasing interest rates. These layers interact in complex ways and potentially can lead to very different outcomes. The distinction between scenarios emerges when we consider uncertainties that could resolve in more than one way.

We call the cross-roads at which Scenario A and Scenario B part company and we go one way or the other a turning point. This may be some years ahead and as yet we cannot tell what will come to pass. A further component of scenarios is discontinuity. Not all unfolding changes are smooth curves. There are jumps after which the world can never be the same again. An example of this was the collapse of the Berlin Wall and all that it implied.

There is no mechanistic way to use these components to assemble scenarios. They are created through a combination of research, analysis, hard thinking and imagination. They involve the skills of the story teller as well as the strategist.

Overview of Scenario Construction

The main stages of working with scenarios are:

1. Clarify the Decision Area
What is the step or decision I am faced with that is affected by uncertainty?

2. Develop Alternative Plots
Given the inevitables, trends and uncertainties, what are the different story plots that might unfold from the current situation?

3. Create Stories of the Future
Given the different possible plots, what are the interesting and challenging stories which context the chosen decision area?

4. Elaborate the Underlying Logics
What are the deeper structures and systems behind the scenario stories that explain them and reveal their crucial differences?

5. Identify Turning Points
Given that no one story is afforded more weight than another, what are the key events that would channel the future towards one scenario rather than another?

In this manual we provide guidance especially in Stages 1 - 3.

It is helpful in working through these stages to bear in mind that scenario construction has a feel of playwriting about it. Using the metaphor of the theatre we can relate the process to the imagination more easily. A good story is also a good drama. The inevitables are like the stage. They are a constant underpinning to all the scenarios. The trends, interplaying with each other, are like the scenes in a play. Their configuration will change with each phase of the unfolding story. The uncertainties are the factors that create the drama and keep us in suspense as to what is going to happen.

How Scenarios are Built

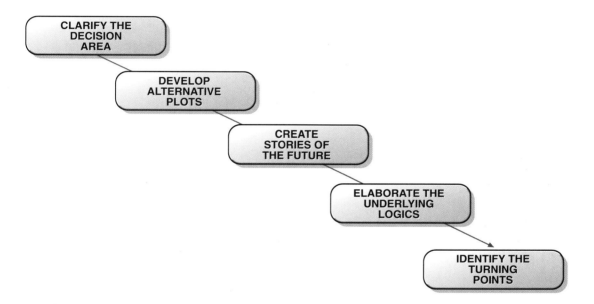

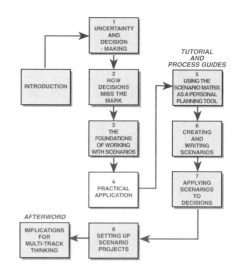

Chapter Four

PRACTICAL APPLICATION

- **The Role of Facilitation**
- **Guidelines for Facilitation**
- **Basic Assumptions Affecting Facilitation**
- **The Working Environment**

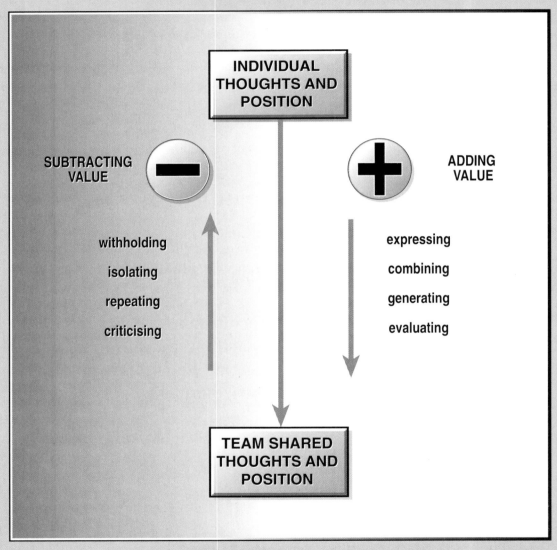

"*Facilitation is the art of helping teams to achieve high performance in their thinking and decision making.... The facilitator's role is to be a catalyst : he or she adds value by activating and stimulating the process without taking the decision power.*"

CHAPTER FOUR

PRACTICAL APPLICATION

The Role of Facilitation

We are all aware of the importance of good teamwork but the challenge to innovate and implement new approaches, whether it be in the generation of strategies or the solution of operational problems, is increasing, with the emphasis being on continual improvement. To meet these new challenges a greater responsibility is placed on effective team or group participation. In turn, new ways of working together are required, stimulated by knowledge and new insight. The idonic modelling process supports this in a memorable and actionable team forum.

Facilitation Acknowledges
Three Areas of Uncertainty

- the outcome of the task is unknown
- the thinking is open-ended
- the interaction is unpredictable

Facilitation is the art of helping teams to achieve high performance in their thinking and decision-making. It can apply to a broad variety of management tasks of which scenario creation is but one.

The facilitator's role is to be a catalyst: he or she adds value by activating and stimulating the process without taking the decision power. Performing this role effectively is one of the key challenges facing us.

Facilitation can support any meeting, ranging from a small group of people to a large conference and may include the setting up, designing and reporting process of the event or series of sessions.

In the facilitation of shared thinking, ideas are captured visually onto idons as they are contributed by participants and worked through the stages of a modelling sequence. At each stage of the process the group's thinking is reflected back to them with the option of making changes if need be, to correspond to a new pattern of thought or insight. The tangible result of the session is a model or series of models that capture both the outcomes and, if using the 'Idons-For-Thinking™' software, a full report of the thinking that has ensued. The output can then be evaluated, built on or integrated into future work.

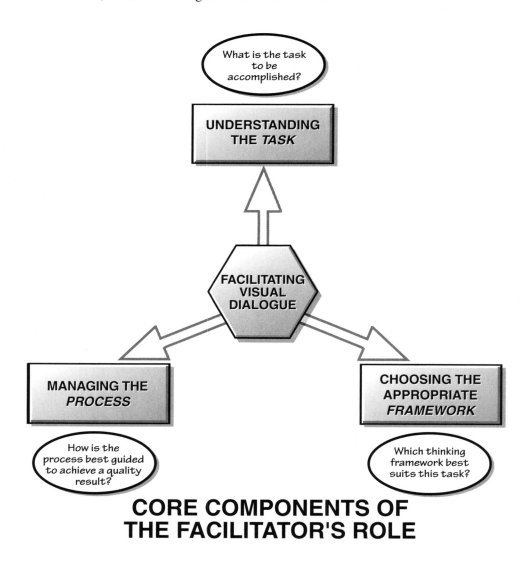

CORE COMPONENTS OF
THE FACILITATOR'S ROLE

Selection of participants is decided according to need, which may range from a pre-selected or established group working on a project, to individuals chosen to contribute diverse views and insights. If the team-work goes well, each member will contribute useful ideas and information. Members' contributions will spark off new ideas and through this process powerful new (shared) insights are created.

Discovery Through Insightful Communication

In traditional meetings we often find that team-work does not get off the ground. For all sorts of reasons, individuals withhold knowledge and keep themselves isolated. Because no new ideas are sparked off, the same material keeps being circulated and no real progress is made. Whoever has the power or has the loudest voice will determine the decision but ownership and implementation are, not surprisingly, weak.

In facilitated meetings the primary role of the facilitator is to help the whole team surface and voice the issues so as to achieve the positive trend which leads to sharing and mutual improvement of understanding. The tools available to the facilitator and the degree of skill he/she has in applying them helps to achieve this. Facilitation is the art of increasing the practical learning of a group working on a task. It has to be done "on-line" as a process of discovery. It is the participation in an immediate "drama" of exploration supported by the team-work. From this point of view the value of a session may be as much in the insights gained as in the output of plans.

The Facilitator as Catalyst

To stimulate the emergence of new ideas, it is necessary to work with ideas produced by the team itself. The facilitator acts as a catalyst for this process because it is very difficult for those involved in a task to remain detached enough to guide the process. At the same time the facilitator generally needs to have some knowledge of the area of concern.

Functional Integration

Another role of facilitation is to help the group create a common language between the members so that real thinking can be shared. Complex challenges require many angles of vision and these may be provided by the various functional expertises in the organisation. It is not always easy to get different functions working together but skilled facilitation provides a soft threshold for this integration.

The Facilitator's Role

The role of Facilitator is a specific one played by a selected person, who brings to bear a variety of skills to assist the group through the modelling process. Sensitivity to the complexity of the task as well as the group dynamics needs to be matched with the competence and skill of the facilitator.

The facilitator has to make sure that the output of the process meets the needs of the team.

A facilitator is needed for the following input :

- to help the group suspend judgement
- to pace the meeting
- to draw a distinction between useful excursions and irrelevancies
- to record or manage the recording of points onto idons
- to guide the group through the underlying stages of modelling
- to provoke new thought by specific idonic modelling techniques.

The facilitator does not command or lead the group but keeps it balanced and on track.

Skilled Facilitation

A good facilitator will have strong concentration capabilities, the capacity to listen deeply and an enquiring mind. In addition he or she will need a flexible and varied approach to thinking and the capacity to stimulate and include contributions.

Competent facilitation requires skills in three key areas:
- understanding the challenge
- using the methods appropriately
- handling the dynamics of the group

As in any craft, a person's ability to use idonic methods and skills effectively will improve with practice over time.

Guidelines For Facilitation

Create a Brief
Create a brief that will specify the main requirements of the workshop.

Design the Process
A process will need to be designed to provide a framework that will focus and trigger the necessary thinking process that will take people through an interaction towards delivering the objective. Your considerations in this should include: the number of people involved; the overall duration of the project; how each stage of the process can be improved upon by applying specific facilitation methods and skills; what are the sensitive points that must be taken into account.

How you have structured the stages of the process has a strong effect on your outcome. A carefully-prepared process will help the group explore all sides of the task and create a high energy flow. The recommended process for the creation and writing of scenarios with a group is offered in Chapter Six of this publication.

Skills Needed During Facilitation

Listening

The facilitator provides an important feedback loop through his or her skills at listening :
- focus and maintain your attention
- take a flexible perspective
- use the speaker's words wherever possible
- be gentle when questioning for clarification

When Capturing Ideas:

- have the speaker summarise his or her point as a title for the hexagon
- offer helpful suggestions if necessary
- do not resist criticism that you have not quite caught the meaning
- take down notes where a summary might be misread later
- invite elaboration where necessary; a headline may not be adequate
- where necessary let the person speak at length and then summarise the thought

Basic Assumptions Affecting Facilitation

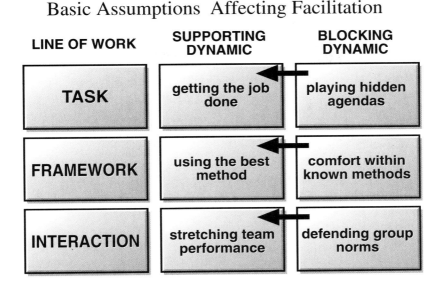

LINE OF WORK	SUPPORTING DYNAMIC	BLOCKING DYNAMIC
TASK	getting the job done	playing hidden agendas
FRAMEWORK	using the best method	comfort within known methods
INTERACTION	stretching team performance	defending group norms

Keeping The Flow Going

If you have designed your process well with the stages built logically on from each other, you will find it is now easier to keep a positive flow. If during facilitation time constraints become an issue, focus on the quality of contact and penetration of the issues being dealt with, rather than comprehensive coverage. If it is important, the coverage can come in post-workshop activity or more time should be allocated. (Correctly structuring timing is important in the design stages.)

Managing The Group Dynamics

However objective a thinking process might appear to be, subjective undercurrents of feeling and value judgement from within the group, which the group itself may not be aware of, may be distorting its objectivity. A skilled facilitator will be aware of this and can steer the group out of its most unproductive dynamics, which if allowed to continue would block effective team-work.

Sometimes a group can be pretty much in agreement over the brainstormed ideas and it is only when challenged, for example when clustering in hexagon modelling, that people begin to shock each other with their different perspectives. These differences of viewpoint, properly discussed, can be a powerful source of new insights. Any new points triggered at this stage need to be captured for later feedback into the process.

Sometimes having the opportunity to share thinking in a group will have a strong opening-up effect on the participants and people become extremely interested in following through each other's deeper level thinking. Your designed exercise may then seem distracting or trivial, even though it was responsible for triggering the process. Recognise the tremendous contribution to team building and team alignment this can give and the implications for team effectiveness. It may be important to progress the group towards the goal, in which case both skill and sensitivity are needed.

New Issues Uncovered
The unique conjunction of perspectives brought out at the workshop may surface an issue which so far has not appeared in the preparatory work. This may change the course of action but it is not a negative result. It might save a business!

A Few Additional Do's and Don'ts

Do...
- prepare adequately for the event, including the room
- make the 'rules of the game' clear
- inform/prepare participants on the issue in question in advance
- be prepared to assist and energise the group when they get stuck
- take some time to extract the learning from each event

Don't...
- write illegibly
- distort meaning when summarising wording
- let negativity split the sharing of mental models
- let the group bog down in detail, drift or lose sight of the outputs
- avoid the issue of probing for better meaning

Facilitation then, involves the use of open-ended methods and a wide range of skills. Having a competent facilitator trained in idonic visual methods will definitely optimise the results of any group session.

The Working Environment For Modelling

The quality of facilitation is very dependent on the environment. Part of the difficulty under normal office and meeting conditions is that either room settings are designed for presentations (say in an auditorium) or for conversations (usually around a boardroom-style table). Even dedicated training rooms with modular furniture are still mainly geared for an audience facing one way in fixed positions.

The environment sets the tone of the meeting and influences the flow of exchange we need to create for facilitation. Even though we largely have to make do with whatever is at hand, we can make some changes. However, this often leads to a battle with furniture that shouldn't be overlooked! Allow time beforehand to plan and re-organise.

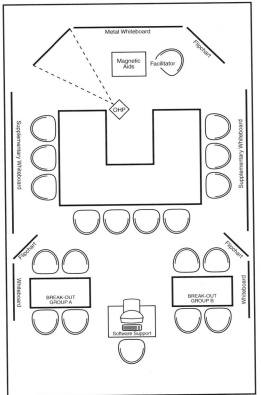

Some useful guiding principles are:

• ensure all participants can have eye contact with each other

• ensure comfortable but "alert" seating with freedom to move around easily. An open circle is best with primary visual aids at the open end of the circle ensuring ease of readability for everyone

• allocate extra space to allow for surrounding the team with whiteboards which accumulate the products of each stage of the workshop and which can therefore be referred to as and when needed

• make space for a computer-support facilitator to work at the rear of the group to capture the output of the workshop (using the 'Idons-For-Thinking™' software)

• note that availability of a data projector can be useful where review of the output as a team is important for the result

Ensuring The Supportive Tools

In visual facilitation with idons, the use of the appropriate media for capturing and representing the conversation and ideas of a team at work is crucial.

The following are recommended:

- several large steel whiteboards with Idon hexagon kits
- flip charts
- overhead projector (occasional use)
- computer with the 'Idons-For-Thinking™' software (for capture, tracking and feedback documentation)

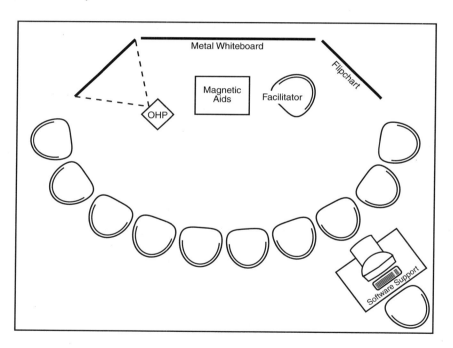

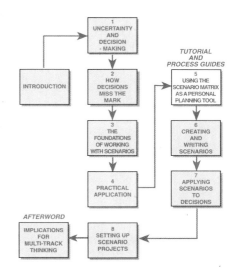

Chapter Five

USING THE SCENARIO MATRIX
AS A PERSONAL PLANNING TOOL
(Tutorial)

- **Introduction**
- **A Personal Scenario Thinking Exercise**

Take a Break and Get a Fresh Perspective

	FUTURE 1	FUTURE 2	FUTURE 3	
PRIORITIES OPTIONS	Unavoidable house repairs	Airlines on strike	New discounts for foreign travel	**ROBUST OPTIONS**
1 Go somewhere totally new for me	Stay: look at home situation in a fresh way	Drive: some local places not explored	Fly: really want to go to high mountains	1 Clear my mind before choosing
2 Do I go alone?	No: be with my partner	Nice to have company	Partner doesn't like flying	2 Ask what he/she thinks is best
3 How much time off can I take?	Maximum: no travel	Allow two days for driving?	Must fly or too short a time	3 Need two weeks if travelling
	Drop my usual "at home" habits	Choose a centre to tour from	Investigate Nepal	
	SOUND ACTION 1	**SOUND ACTION 2**	**SOUND ACTION 3**	

CHAPTER FIVE

USING THE SCENARIO MATRIX
AS A PERSONAL PLANNING TOOL

Introduction

Uncertainty about the future is not a new issue - but what we may be experiencing as new is an acceleration in the changes in our personal lives and in the workplace. The unknowns affect very directly our future planning for ourselves and our families. This appears to be a time when the range of forces and knowledge impacting on us makes us question our interpretations of life, relationships, the nature of business, ethics, values, security and even survival. We may even feel we need a radical re-frame and this can be daunting - unless we realise that this may in fact be no more than a new understanding: a clarification and guiding framework to empower the way forward.

In this light, the ability to do multi-future thinking provides us with a degree of informed destiny control and enables us to navigate through the developing unknown.

It is essential, therefore, to practise the art of multi-future thinking as often as possible in order to develop our cognitive capacity. This section introduces you to a simple and direct framework that will enable you to do this. Also, when working in a group, the outcome is always far more powerful and effective if the individuals involved in the shared thinking have already acquired some degree of this cognitive flexibility.

A Personal Scenario Thinking Exercise

Preparations
This technique is best done in a quiet environment where you can work undisturbed with the Idon personal magnetic Scenario Kit or a pc with Idons-For-Thinking™ software.

You Need
Different coloured rectangles in the proportions that follow, in colours of your choice. For the purposes of this tutorial we have used three red, three green, two violet, two blue and two brown. You also need nine rectangles of another colour - we have used yellow. When using magnetics, you will need a metal-backed whiteboard or Liteboard™.

The Topic of Concern
Step 1
Identify an issue of current concern to you and make a note of it on your modelling surface. The example we give here is "Take a Break and Get a Fresh Perspective".

Identifying Priority Actions
Step 2
To begin your modelling, place three red rectangles one above the other on your modelling surface like this:

Take a Break and Get a Fresh Perspective

Step 3

What do you see as a major priority or needed action in this area? Summarise your thoughts and write them into the first rectangle like this example.

Take a Break and Get a Fresh Perspective

Step 4

Now think of the second most important priority, needed action, option or consideration to do with this same area of concern. It should be something that needs to be taken into account to ensure a good outcome. Summarise this in the second rectangle and then complete the third rectangle in the same way with your third priority concern.

Take a Break and Get a Fresh Perspective

Setting up the Framework
Step 5
To the right of each of the rectangles on your modelling surface, place three more rectangles, this time coloured yellow, to form an array that looks like this:

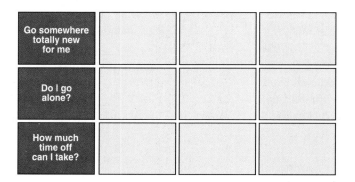

Take a Break and Get a Fresh Perspective

Step 6
Now place one violet, one blue and one brown rectangle in a horizontal row above the nine yellow ones.

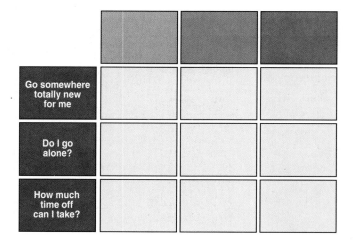

Take a Break and Get a Fresh Perspective

Take a Break and Get a Fresh Perspective

Identifying Different Futures
Step 7

Formulate three possible views of the future which will affect your choices. The scenarios should include factors outside of your control. They should be as distinct as possible. Write the first in the violet, the second in the blue and the third in the brown rectangle. You will be seeing how your actions in the priority areas of concern will change in each of these different futures.

	Unavoidable house repairs	Airlines on strike	New discounts for foreign travel
Go somewhere totally new for me			
Do I go alone?			
How much time off can I take?			

Take a Break and Get a Fresh Perspective

Exploring Potential Actions
Step 8

You will see an intersection between each scenario and each of your priorities, concerns or initiatives. Choosing your first priority, ask yourself what you would do about that priority in that future scenario. Sum up your thinking and write it onto the yellow rectangle positioned at the intersection.

	Unavoidable house repairs	Airlines on strike	New discounts for foreign travel
Go somewhere totally new for me	Stay: look at home situation in a fresh way		
Do I go alone?			
How much time off can I take?			

Take a Break and Get a Fresh Perspective

	Unavoidable house repairs	Airlines on strike	New discounts for foreign travel
Go somewhere totally new for me	Stay: look at home situation in a fresh way		
Do I go alone?	No: be with my partner		
How much time off can I take?	Maximum: no travel		

Step 9

Go to your next priority or option and ask yourself what you would do about it in that same future world. Note down your thinking on this also, then finish with the third yellow rectangle in the column.

Take a Break and Get a Fresh Perspective

	Unavoidable house repairs	Airlines on strike	New discounts for foreign travel
Go somewhere totally new for me	Stay: look at home situation in a fresh way	Drive: some local places not explored	Fly: really want to go to high mountains
Do I go alone?	No: be with my partner	Nice to have company	Partner doesn't like flying
How much time off can I take?	Maximum: no travel	Allow two days for driving?	Must fly or too short a time

Step 10

Repeat the process for each of the remaining intersections until you have completed all three yellow columns.

Considering Robustness
Step 11
Now look again at your first priority or option, review your summations of its impact in the different futures (yellow rectangles) and ask yourself what the implications are for making this priority more robust in the light of these possible different futures? Where might you need to correct your thinking for any assumptions that only one of those futures might happen?

Take a green rectangle and place it at the end of the row to the right of the three yellow rectangles. Write your summation on it as in this example.

Take a Break and Get a Fresh Perspective

	Unavoidable house repairs	Airlines on strike	New discounts for foreign travel	
Go somewhere totally new for me	Stay: look at home situation in a fresh way	Drive: some local places not explored	Fly: really want to go to high mountains	Clear my mind before choosing
Do I go alone?	No: be with my partner	Nice to have company	Partner doesn't like flying	
How much time off can I take?	Maximum: no travel	Allow two days for driving?	Must fly or too short a time	

Step 12
Repeat this process for the remaining two priorities or options.

Take a Break and Get a Fresh Perspective

	Unavoidable house repairs	Airlines on strike	New discounts for foreign travel	
Go somewhere totally new for me	Stay: look at home situation in a fresh way	Drive: some local places not explored	Fly: really want to go to high mountains	Clear my mind before choosing
Do I go alone?	No: be with my partner	Nice to have company	Partner doesn't like flying	Ask what he/she thinks is best
How much time off can I take?	Maximum: no travel	Allow two days for driving?	Must fly or too short a time	Need two weeks if travelling

Identifying Sound Action
Step 13
Now look at your three priorities or options and the actions you have identified to enable you to implement them in your first future scenario (yellow rectangles). Ask yourself what your best overall course of action is, accommodating all three options, in the first future or "scenario".

Sum this up and write it into a violet rectangle and position it as below:

Take a Break and Get a Fresh Perspective

	Unavoidable house repairs	Airlines on strike	New discounts for foreign travel	
Go somewhere totally new for me	Stay: look at home situation in a fresh way	Drive: some local places not explored	Fly: really want to go to high mountains	Clear my mind before choosing
Do I go alone?	No: be with my partner	Nice to have company	Partner doesn't like flying	Ask what he/she thinks is best
How much time off can I take?	Maximum: no travel	Allow two days for driving?	Must fly or too short a time	Need two weeks if travelling
	Drop my usual "at home" habits			

Completing the Matrix
Step 14
Place a blue rectangle next to the violet and lastly a brown one next to the blue to form a row at the bottom. Repeat the above process for the remaining two scenarios and sum up your thinking in the blue and brown rectangles to complete the matrix.

Take a Break and Get a Fresh Perspective

	Unavoidable house repairs	Airlines on strike	New discounts for foreign travel	
Go somewhere totally new for me	Stay: look at home situation in a fresh way	Drive: some local places not explored	Fly: really want to go to high mountains	Clear my mind before choosing
Do I go alone?	No: be with my partner	Nice to have company	Partner doesn't like flying	Ask what he/she thinks is best
How much time off can I take?	Maximum: no travel	Allow two days for driving?	Must fly or too short a time	Need two weeks if travelling
	Drop my usual "at home" habits	Choose a centre to tour from	Investigate Nepal	

You have now created your own personal scenario matrix which will help you decide your next steps. You may wish to take a few minutes to consider what has happened as a result of the exercise and assimilate the implications and guidelines for robustness irrespective of which future comes into being.

Remember to re-visit the matrix as further information becomes available.

This technique of adjusting your priorities and actions flexibly towards unknown futures or scenarios accelerates your capacity to do multi-future thinking and will greatly enhance your ability to contribute to a group scenario process when working with others.

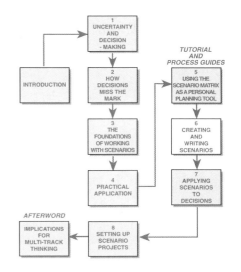

Chapter Six

CREATING AND WRITING SCENARIOS WITH A GROUP
(Process Guide)

- **Clarifying Environmental Factors**
- **Creating Prototype Scenarios**
- **Generating Multiple Images of the Future**
- **Verifying Through Environmental Scanning**
- **Where We Are Now in the Process**

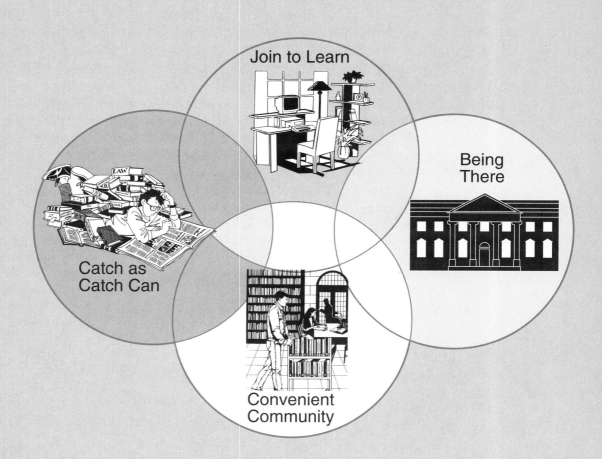

Join to Learn

Being
There

Catch as
Catch Can

Convenient
Community

CHAPTER SIX

CREATING AND WRITING SCENARIOS WITH A GROUP

Clarifying Environmental Factors

Scenarios are constructed from a varied background of knowledge and guess-work about the wider environment and the trends and discontinuities likely in the future. Well-rounded scenarios draw on both the research and the opinions of a diverse set of people from different walks of life. Some of the dimensions that might be covered in this wider environment are:

- research and technology
- institutional and market trends
- social values and life-styles
- economic futures
- management and delivery systems
- ethical and value questions
- global political influences
- ecological/environmental issues

One way to provide this variety is to create scenarios with a representative diverse group of people. Each person will have priority concerns that he/she will consider as important issues to be built into the scenarios. Gathering this diversity creates a rich "lego kit" of factors from which to construct scenarios. It can be difficult to see how to move from such a set of "factors" to actually constructing scenarios. The Idon technique which follows is a good way to do this.

A Note About Software Capture

Throughout the exercises that follow it is recommended that comments and explanations about the meaning behind the necessarily abbreviated contents of the idons be captured in the 'Notes' function of the Idons-For-Thinking™ software. This ensures that the group's thinking is available for future reference and provides a rich database of information from which the scenario stories can be written up in a narrative form for effective communication to others.

Purpose
The purpose of this technique is to examine and evaluate a set of wider environmental factors, ambiguities and uncertainties volunteered by a group in order to resolve which role they are likely to play in the unfolding of a variety of scenarios.

The Worked Example
In order to illustrate the stages of the method, an example application has been chosen.

Imagine a group of educational administrators meeting to consider the changes taking place in society, the impact of new information technologies and how their future policies need to evolve. They have chosen a scenario method and are now embarking on the creation of a set of challenging scenarios.

Preparations
This technique is best done on a metal-backed whiteboard, preferably in a supportive environment for group work as outlined in Chapter 4.

You need
- *a large metal-backed whiteboard (6' x 4' is good)*
- *a set of about 40 magnetic hexagons* (4.5" or 6", depending on the size of the group)*
- *dry-wipe pens*
- *a duster for cleaning idons and board as needed*
- *a PC with Idons-For-Thinking™ software*

* see Appendix.

The Facilitation Steps

Step 1 - Gathering Factors
The facilitator formulates a question designed to elicit responses from participants which will cover the area of concern chosen by the group. This is called the "Trigger Question" because it triggers thoughts about the subject in hand.

For our example we have chosen the following Trigger Question:

"Looking at the wider environment of education, what do you see as the most important external factors that will determine the priorities for education?"

The facilitator writes down contributions from participants onto hexagons and collects them on the whiteboard, numbering them in sequence as they emerge. These gathered factors can be defined as 'uncertainties'- factors we are concerned about but not sure of.

These are the factors from our example group:

Important Factors Determining Priorities for Education

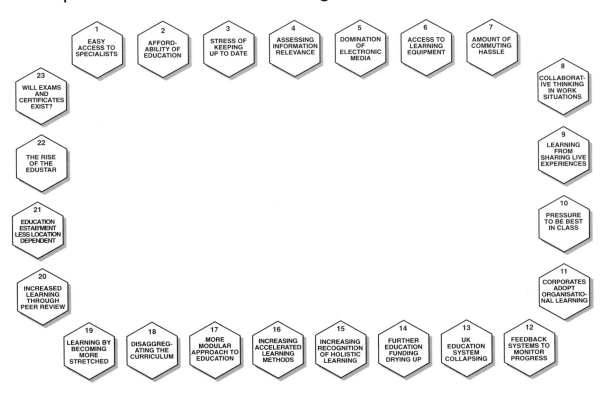

Step 2 - Positioning on the Grid

Te next step is to sort the factors according to their degree of uncertainty and how direct their impact is likely to be on priorities. The visual method here is to use a two-dimensional grid.

The dimensions of the grid are introduced, without interpretation at this point. The idea here is to begin to sort the different factors, placing them on the grid where the participants feel they best belong. Each factor is taken in turn and its position discussed and provisionally fixed according to its perceived "Higher" or "Lower" Uncertainty and "Indirect" and "Direct" Impact on our organisation. Note that absolute positioning is not the point; it is relative positioning that is important.

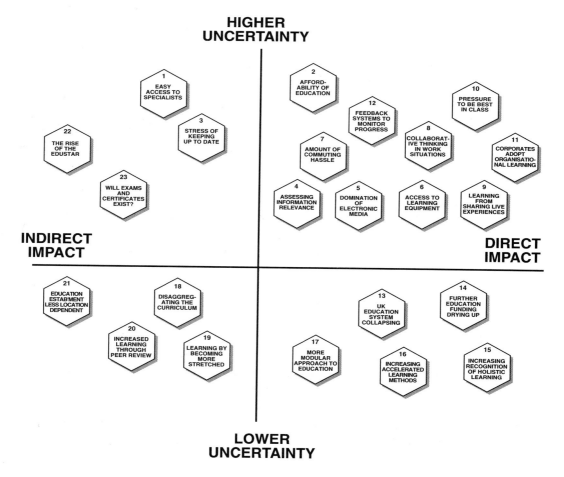

Step 3 - Survey All Factors

When all the factors have been placed in position, the whole set is reviewed by the group and fine adjustments made in relative positioning.

The example on the previous page shows how our group has positioned its factors on the grid.

Step 4 - Characterise the Quadrants

The facilitator explains that each quadrant has a different interpretation but that there is no sharp line of distinction either vertical or horizontal. The behaviour of the factors is discussed as:

Top right: pivotal uncertainties

These are likely to have a direct impact but their outcome is uncertain. They are pivotal in the sense that the way they turn out may have strong directional consequences. These are the areas that will determine the shape of different scenarios.

Top left: potential jokers

These are pretty uncertain as to their outcome and less relevant. However, it could be dangerous to treat them as merely noise. They represent factors to monitor on the 'corporate radar' in case they move strongly to the right.

Bottom right: significant trends

These impact more directly on our situation and it should be possible to anticipate their effect.

Bottom left: context shapers

These are relatively certain and therefore will surely shape the future context.

Overleaf is how our example model looks at this stage in the process.

Use of the Other Three Quadrants

In the exercise that follows we are going to use the uncertainties from the "pivotal uncertainties" quadrant. The uncertainties collected in the other quadrants are usually retained for reference and inclusion in the final stages of writing up scenarios in the following ways:

- The factors in the context shapers quadrant are those that should be woven into every scenario if it is written up fully.

- The significant trends will also run through each scenario but the manner in which they manifest will be diferent in each one.
- The potential jokers are useful factors to bring into a scenario if the facilitator feels that what is developing is too close to the default scenario.

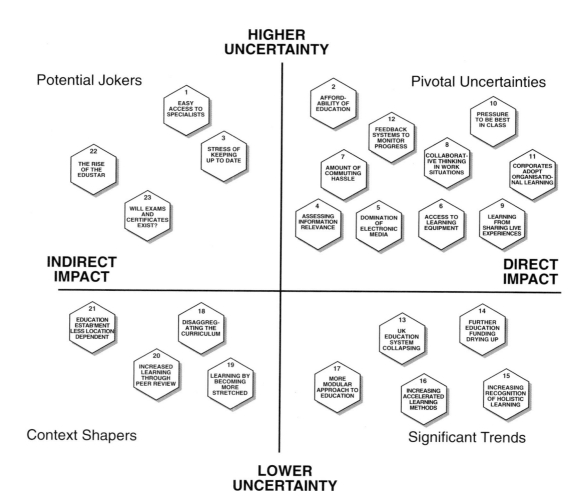

HIGHER UNCERTAINTY

Potential Jokers

Pivotal Uncertainties

1 EASY ACCESS TO SPECIALISTS

2 AFFORD-ABILITY OF EDUCATION

10 PRESSURE TO BE BEST IN CLASS

3 STRESS OF KEEPING UP TO DATE

12 FEEDBACK SYSTEMS TO MONITOR PROGRESS

22 THE RISE OF THE EDUSTAR

8 COLLABORAT-IVE THINKING IN WORK SITUATIONS

11 CORPORATES ADOPT ORGANISATIO-NAL LEARNING

7 AMOUNT OF COMMUTING HASSLE

23 WILL EXAMS AND CERTIFICATES EXIST?

4 ASSESSING INFORMATION RELEVANCE

5 DOMINATION OF ELECTRONIC MEDIA

6 ACCESS TO LEARNING EQUIPMENT

9 LEARNING FROM SHARING LIVE EXPERIENCES

INDIRECT IMPACT

DIRECT IMPACT

21 EDUCATION ESTAB'MENT LESS LOCATION DEPENDENT

18 DISAGGREG-ATING THE CURRICULUM

14 FURTHER EDUCATION FUNDING DRYING UP

13 UK EDUCATION SYSTEM COLLAPSING

20 INCREASED LEARNING THROUGH PEER REVIEW

19 LEARNING BY BECOMING MORE STRETCHED

17 MORE MODULAR APPROACH TO EDUCATION

16 INCREASING ACCELERATED LEARNING METHODS

15 INCREASING RECOGNITION OF HOLISTIC LEARNING

Context Shapers

Significant Trends

LOWER UNCERTAINTY

Creating Prototype Scenarios

Scenarios can be thought of simply as having three levels. At the base level there are the context shapers which seem pretty inevitable and will tend to underpin all scenarios at a given time - these are changes that are common throughout, like the *stage* in a theatre.

At the intermediate level there are trends and these can be quite complex because of the variety of ways they can interact with each other. These will be modified from scenario to scenario but still retain their basic condition These can be likened to the changing *scenery* in a play.

At the differentiated level each scenario has some unique variances. These differences arise from the uncertainties we perceive. An uncertainty about something means at least things could "go this way or go that way". Uncertainties may be main line or they may be jokers or wild cards.

As these uncertainties interact in different ways that affect how things turn out, the combinations of even twenty variables are astronomic. We need a way to simplify this information, without diluting its impact, into different emergent stories of the future. These may be perceived as the different *dramas* that might be put on in a theatre. In order to do this we go through the following stages in creating prototype scenarios from which a full set of scenarios can be developed.

We have chosen here a way to generate four contrasting scenarios.

Purpose
The purpose of this technique is to work with the pivotal uncertainties box of the environmental factors grid to create simple scenarios that bring out distinct future challenges.

Preparations
This technique is best done on a metal-backed whiteboard, preferably in a supportive environment for group work as outlined in Chapter 4.

You need
- a large metal-backed whiteboard (6' x 4' is good)
- a set of about 30 magnetic hexagons* (4.5" or 6", depending on the size of the group)

- dry-wipe pens
- a duster for cleaning idons and board as needed
- a PC with Idons-For-Thinking™ software

* see Appendix.

Step 1 - Reframing The Pivotal Uncertainties as Questions

Looking at the factors in the quadrant marked "pivotal uncertainties", participants are invited to think of each one as an uncertainty question for which there are at least two possible outcomes. Although there may be several outcomes, for this exercise we confine it to a choice of two contrasting ones. We will call an outcome state the "flip" (e.g "Yes, education will be affordable") and the other contrasting outcome state the "flop" (e.g. "No, education will not be affordable"). When the factor in question has either "flipped" or "flopped", the uncertainty is resolved.

Participants are invited to reframe each factor as a question, then take fresh hexagons and write the reframed factors on them, placing them on a new whiteboard surface. It can be helpful to write the numbers previously allocated to the issues on the board under each new hexagon. For example, beneath "Will Education Be Affordable?" we can write the number 2, referring to the hexagon in the previous model entitled "Affordability of Education".

This is how our educational group might reframe their questions:

Pivotal Uncertainties
Reframed as Questions

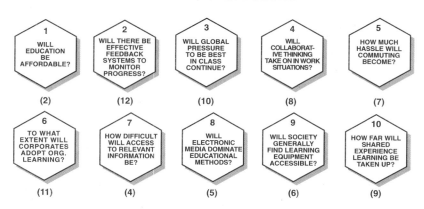

Step 2 - Grouping the Uncertainties

The facilitator invites the group to come up and work with the hexagons on the board, searching for connections and associations between the uncertainties. Connections are expressed by linking the hexagons together. Uncertainty areas connect because of the impact of their influence on each other, either because if one "flips" the other will be made to "flop", or because they are likely to align by association. This is a kind of "domino effect". The facilitator will need to guide this process towards achieving consolidation into two main clusters or at least two priority clusters out of a set. He/she can help this process by:

- encouraging people to avoid simple classification grouping
- asking any person placing two hexagons together to briefly explain the link for the benefit of group understanding
- encouraging brief discussion of differences of viewpoint where people disagree but moving on if there is no quick resolution
- explaining that aiming for two clusters is a device to focus on for later scenario creating and need not be laboured over too strongly

In the following example, the uncertainties have been grouped into two clusters:

Grouping the Uncertainties

CLUSTER **A**

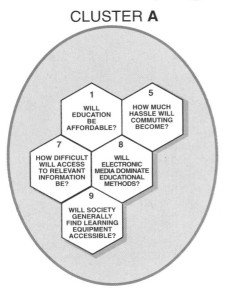

CLUSTER **B**

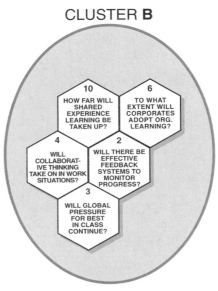

Step 3 - Naming the Sub Plots

In the clusters we now have groups of questions. When one of the uncertainty questions resolves to, say, a "flip" side, it will tend to correlate with the "flip" side of all the other uncertainties in that cluster. This will end up resolving the entire cluster as a large scale "flip" or "flop". It is rather like a group of little magnets organising themselves to a main N-pole and S-pole.

For example, in the first cluster we might suppose that:

BIG FLIP **AI**		BIG FLOP **A2**
	Hexagon	
• education affordable	(1)	• education difficult to afford
• easy access to information	(7)	• difficult to access information
• electronic media dominates	(8)	• traditional media retained
• commuting increasingly difficult	(5)	• mobility still easy
• access to learning equipment	(9)	• equipment only for the few
leads to the name:		leads to the name:
REMOTE LEARNING		**LOCAL LEARNING**

In the second cluster we might suppose the following:

BIG FLIP **BI**		BIG FLOP **B2**
	Hexagon	
• emphasis on individual learning	(10)	• emphasis on shared learning
• no take-up of organisational learning	(6)	• adoption of organisational learning
• minimal collaboration	(4)	• collaborative thinking at work
• poor feedback systems	(2)	• effective feedback system
• global pressure reducing	(3)	• global pressure for best in class
leads to the name:		leads to the name:
INDIVIDUALISM DOMINATES		**CORPORATISM DOMINATES**

The two outcomes of the whole cluster are called sub-plots, which will combine in different ways to give us different scenarios.

The facilitator draws two arrows coming out of each cluster and works with the group to give each arrow a name that characterises the combined variables in the cluster in one of two directions. Each "name" needs to express a coherent alternative view of the combined uncertainties - more than simply "good" or "bad" but suggestive of how things might develop. They should be imaginative and evocative, like good chapter headings of a novel.

The facilitator should:
- invite members to contribute suggestions for each main arrow
- use the version that attracts most energy and consensus in the group
- if they are stuck, be creative
- finally, encourage the group to give the clusters themselves an overall theme title for easy identification

Below is an example of sub-plots from the clusters in the example model:

Naming the Sub-Plots

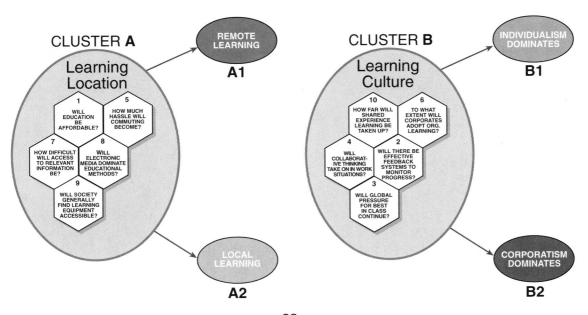

Generating Multiple Images of the Future

When sub-plots have been generated using the hexagon cluster "flip-flop" method, they need to be combined to form scenario structures. On the one hand this is a logical process in which there are a set number of combinations statistically. On the other hand it is an intense exercise of imagination and judgement where the participants are challenged to synthesise each set of combinations to formulate scenario stories which are stimulating and relevant to the thinking task.

By using the table technique here it is possible to manage the logical combination process together with the stimulus to the imagination.

Purpose
The purpose of this technique is to arrive at creating four scenarios generated from the two clusters, each of which has two states or sub-plots. The titles of these scenarios will represent four distinct possible futures extrapolated from the thinking done by the group and will hold rich meanings which can be further fleshed out when the scenarios are written up after the exercise is completed.

Preparations
This technique requires a 3' x 4' metal-backed whiteboard placed in portrait position and a set of magnetic rectangles (available in the Idon Scenario Kit) in colours of your choice comprising eight of one colour and two each of five other colours. We have chosen as follows:

- 8 yellow
- 2 blue
- 2 silver
- 2 violet
- 2 green
- 2 red

It is also necessary for the models from the previous exercise to be available for reference. Ideally, each participant will have a print-out with accompanying notes produced from Idons-For-Thinking™ software captured from the previous modelling session.

The Facilitation Steps

The facilitator sets up the matrix on the board as shown below, writing the cluster titles from the previous exercise in the red rectangles at the top of the two middle columns.

	CLUSTER **A** (RED)	CLUSTER **B** (RED)
	LEARNING LOCATION	LEARNING CULTURE
YELLOW FOR TITLE	BLUE (A1)	SILVER (B1)
YELLOW FOR TITLE	BLUE (A1)	GREEN (B2)
YELLOW FOR TITLE	VIOLET (A2)	SILVER (B1)
YELLOW FOR TITLE	VIOLET (A2)	GREEN (B2)

Step 1 - Logging the Combinations

The four outcomes from the two clusters can be combined in four different ways to form "images of the future". In our example, if "Remote Learning" is A1, "Local Learning" A2, Individualism Dominates" B1 and "Corporatism Dominates" B2, then the possible combinations are as follows:

A1 + B1
A1 + B2
A2 + B1
A2 + B2

In our matrix, we have chosen the colour Blue for A1, Silver for B1, Violet for A2 and Green for B2.

Now the facilitator needs to:

- write the A1 and B1 flip titles in the first row of rectangles (blue and silver)
- ask people to look again at the combination of flips or flops that form these worlds as in the example BIG FLIP/FLOP tables on Page 82
- encourage people to use their imagination to form a mental picture of the world that emerges
- help people to create a provisional title for that world and put it into the yellow rectangle on the left

In our example, these are the combinations the group is working with:

A1 + B1	Remote Learning + Individualism Dominates
A1 + B2	Remote Learning + Corporatism Dominates
A2 + B1	Local Learning + Individualism Dominates
A2 + B2	Local Learning + Corporatism Dominates

Depending on how much time has elapsed between this exercise and the previous one, there may need to be some discussion amongst the group at this stage to help to jog people's memories as to the thinking behind the hexagon titles in the previous model. Any new insights can be logged on a flipchart or in the "Notes" function of the Idons-For-Thinking™ software.

This exercise requires a creative leap in the minds of the participants and should not be rushed.

Step 2 - Covering the Matrix
With help from the facilitator, the group now needs to:

- repeat the above steps a further three times with the rest of the possible combinations

On the following page is an example of scenario titles that our educational group might have generated:

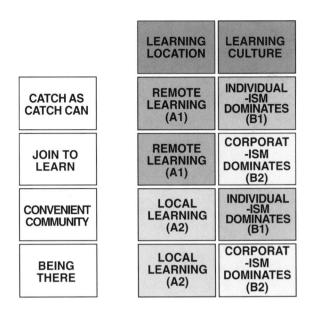

	LEARNING LOCATION	LEARNING CULTURE
CATCH AS CATCH CAN	REMOTE LEARNING (A1)	INDIVIDUAL-ISM DOMINATES (B1)
JOIN TO LEARN	REMOTE LEARNING (A1)	CORPORAT-ISM DOMINATES (B2)
CONVENIENT COMMUNITY	LOCAL LEARNING (A2)	INDIVIDUAL-ISM DOMINATES (B1)
BEING THERE	LOCAL LEARNING (A2)	CORPORAT-ISM DOMINATES (B2)

The result can also be represented as a two dimensional grid creating four scenario spaces like this:

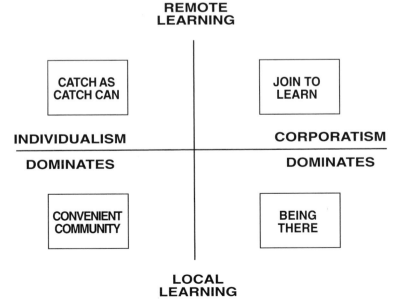

Some people find it useful to elect a spokesperson to stand up at this stage and improvise a 'story' around each title, using the structure as a basis for further write-up afterwards. This has the added value of bringing the prototype scenario stories alive and provides an opportunity for light relief after some tough thinking.

Verifying Through Environmental Scanning

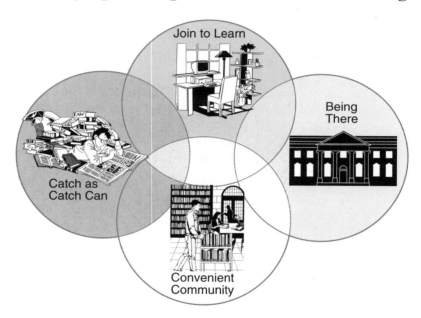

Since scenarios are about the longer range future, usually designed to stretch people's assumptions about what might happen by getting beyond their day-to-day time horizon, it is easy to slip into believing that the scenarios are close to fantasy with no real relevance to the present.

Purpose

The purpose of this technique is to connect people with the perception that any scenario developed in this manner for the long term, will also have current evidence that it is already happening to some degree. This current evidence is what we call *pockets of the future in the present*.

Preparations

This technique is best done on a metal-backed whiteboard, preferably in a supportive environment for group work.

You need
- a large metal-backed whiteboard
- interlocking circles template drawn on the whiteboard
- hexagons* to populate the circles (about 20 of 4.5" or 6", depending on the size of the group)
- coloured dry-wipe pens
- a duster
- a PC with Idons-For-Thinking™ software

* see Appendix.

The Facilitation Steps

Step 1 - Diagram the Scenarios
- Briefly review the scenarios and depict them as four interlocking circles.

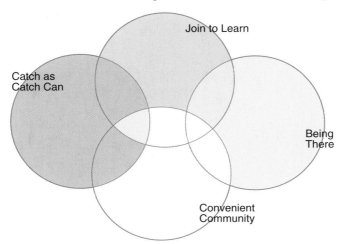

- It is useful to give each scenario a colour code that corresponds to available pen colours.
- An interesting way of involving the group in the circle drawing is to take a poll on

whether the group thinks a scenario is large, medium or small in relation to the others based on current evidence (see page 14).
- The diagram needs to be big so you can populate the overlaps with examples.

Step 2 - Discover Instances
- Point out that stories of the future tend to contain elements that are already with us - pockets of the future in the present. Taking each scenario in turn ask the group to volunteer specific examples that are currently happening somewhere in the world.
- You may need to have researched one or two for each scenario yourself to be sure to trigger people's thinking.
- Be prepared to highlight different aspects of the scenarios to focus the discovery, like "do we know of any instances where x occurred recently?"
- Even a couple of examples per scenario will have the right effect on increasing people's ability to entertain scenarios that they may have had a hard time accepting initially.

Here are some elements our educational group has picked out:

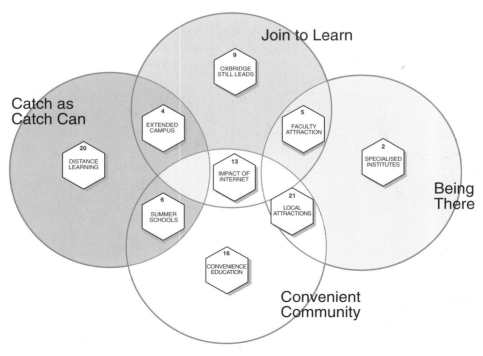

Step 3 - Reinforce Plausibility

- Review the total picture and ask the group to note how the "distant" future is no longer so distant. Relate this experience also to the idea of priming the brain to pick up the signals about the scenarios it might otherwise have missed.
- Review by reading out the instances which seem to be pretty common to all scenarios; these will probably give evidence of the context shapers..
- Review by reading out the examples in each distinct scenario and asking, "What environmental scanning would you do to monitor this aspect?"

Where We Are Now in the Process

You will remember from Chapter 5 that the Scenario Matrix is a way of testing options in different possible futures. The stage we have reached now is to have created four possible futures which can serve as a "wind tunnel" for testing intentions.

However, to return to our educational administrators, they have not yet gone through a process to clarify their decision options. They now have the top row of the matrix but not the left hand column. Chapter 7, which follows, describes and illustrates a way in which a group can rapidly clarify its shared decision intent in a way that can be tested and developed using the scenario matrix. To take the wind tunnel analogy further, we need different airframes to put to the test. And, like aircraft designers, we also need to stimulate new design ideas through the results of these tests.

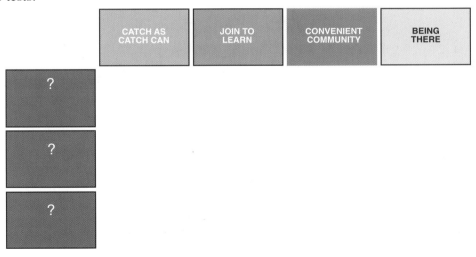

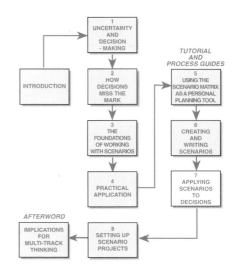

Chapter Seven

APPLYING SCENARIOS TO DECISIONS
(Process Guide)

- **Mapping Decision Issues**
- **Using the Idon Decision/Scenario Matrix**
- **Drawing Conclusions From the Scenario Matrix**
- **Scanning the Present for the Future - Cognitive Priming**

	CATCH AS CATCH CAN	JOIN TO LEARN	CONVENIENT COMMUNITY	BEING THERE	
SET UP COLLABORATIVE EDUCATION VENTURES WITH BUSINESS	DIFFICULT UNLESS NICHED	HIGH APPEAL	FOR LOCAL EMPLOYMENT	ONLY WITH TOP RATING	ESTABLISH A HIGH-VALUE POSITION WITH LOCAL SUPPORT & ROLL-OUT POTENTIAL
PROMOTE AND DEVELOP KNOWLEDGE CENTRE IMAGE	MUST BE GLOBALISED	LINK TO VOCATIONS	NOT SO CRITICAL	CONCENTRATED CENTRES	ACCUMULATE KNOW-LEDGE CONTENT WITH VOCATIONAL RELEVANCE & SEV-ERAL DISTRIBUTION OPTIONS
CULTIVATE A PEOPLE-BASED EDUCATION REPUTATION	NOT MUCH APPEAL	APPRENTICE-SHIP STYLE	LOCAL PROMINENCE	STRONG APPEAL	DEVELOP PEOPLE REPUTATION WITH OPTIONS TO PROMOTE THIS THROUGH MULTI-MEDIA
	REMOTE TUTORING EXPERTISE	DEVELOP VOCATIONAL TRACK RECORD	INVOLVING LOCAL STAKEHOLDERS	BREAKTHROUGH FOR WORLD CLASS PERFORMANCE	

CHAPTER SEVEN

APPLYING SCENARIOS TO DECISIONS

Mapping Decision Issues

There are two main areas of need in mapping decision issues: the team and the stakeholders. This Idon method can help both.

For management teams, the pressure of daily operational tasks coupled with that of producing formalised plans squeezes the time and energy available for serious and creative decision thinking. Where creative decision thinking does go on, it often takes place in isolation rather than in a group process. The piecing together of the bigger picture is frequently done by the Chief Executive, with other team members being mainly occupied with their functional speciality. This means that everyone progresses his/her thinking about what is important without the added value of interaction and the opportunity to bounce ideas off other team members. In this situation the team does not share a mental model of whatever is developing.

Where many stakeholders are concerned, usually there is little scope for involving all the different interested parties who will actually affect implementation in the development of decision issues. The process which follows provides a framework and conduct for discussion in such cases and allows all participants to "own" the resulting thinking. The presence of a trained facilitator, well versed in group dynamics is particularly helpful where a multi-stakeholder group is gathered together.

Purpose
The purpose of this technique is to surface broader options for making decisions that can take into account potential difficulties, developments or opportunities that might occur in the future and see how they interconnect as a whole by creating a mental map. Through discussing the map, participants come closer together in sharing their mental models of strategy and formulate a number of "decision options" which will lead into the next process.

Based on a general decision intent, a decision option is a way of bringing something quite specific into being in the face of multiple possible futures. The real power of any decision option stems from the alignment of understanding and commitment of the people involved in

95

formulating that option. The following technique ensures that alignment.

Preparations
This technique is done on a metal-backed whiteboard, preferably in a supportive environment for group work.

You need
- a large metal-backed whiteboard (6' x 4' is good)
- 30 - 50 magnetic hexagons* (4.5" or 6", depending on the size of the group)
- dry-wipe pens
- a duster
- a PC with Idons-For-Thinking™ software

* see Appendix.

The Facilitation Steps

When faced with a decision challenge, the tendency is to rush into fixing on an option before we have actually grasped the situation. This inevitably leads to partial results and even, on occasions, decisions that actually make the situation worse. Poor decisions that worsen the situation are indications that we may have rushed into an option too quickly and failed to consider all the issues and factors. They may also indicate that we have not sufficiently considered the way factors are interconnected and how interrelationships can be as important for the outcome as the factors themselves. The following method counteracts this risky tendency.

Step 1 - Setting the Trigger Question
- Everyone in the group addresses the following trigger question individually:

    "What do you think are the most important issues that we should be taking into account to be sure of an effective and acceptable way forward?"

Each person makes individual notes without conversation. This is a time for people to do their own reflection. This step also ensures that the value in everyone's thinking is captured and not swept aside by discussion, as can often be the case in a group situation.

Step 2 - Collecting Contributions

- The facilitator asks each person in turn to contribute just one factor. This is written down (summarised if necessary) on a hexagon. Number each hexagon in the top corner in the sequence of generation. This is helpful for easy reference in future steps. The contributor can explain briefly why his/her factor should be included. (Where a 'capture' role is available, these supplementary points can be noted down, for example in the "Notes" function in Idons-For-Thinking™ software).

- The process is repeated until the factors have been collected and arrayed around the whiteboard.

- If there is a duplication, the contributor moves on to the next on his/her list.

- Conversation is restricted by the facilitator to points of clarification. No discussion is allowed at this stage.

- When two or three rounds have been done (depending on the size of the group) then the facilitator takes a more informal approach with a question: "Does anyone have anything left on his/her list which is different from what we have so far?"

Issues in Re-organising Higher Education

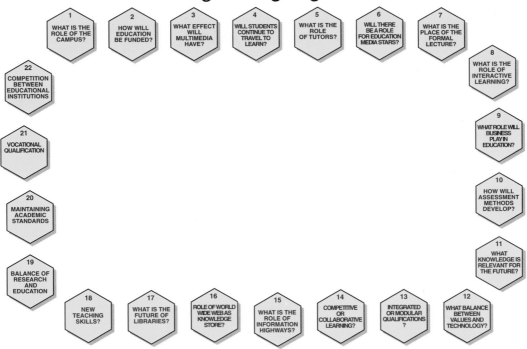

The process is repeated until the factors have been collected and arrayed around the whiteboard.

An example of issues collected from a group working in education is on the previous page.

Step 3 - Clustering

- The hexagons are now studied and connections looked for. Where a connection is seen the hexagons are put together to build a cluster.
- The facilitator encourages people to look for interesting connections rather than simple classification.
- As a general rule, once clusters acquire more than seven or eight hexagons, this is an indication that another sub-cluster needs splitting out to clarify meaning.

In this step, conversation is allowed since people need to discover each other's viewpoints. As conversation progresses, the facilitator guides the focus towards intentions and options in that area.

In the following example, our educational group has clustered their issues thus:

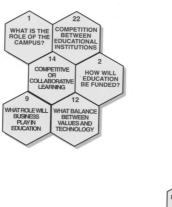

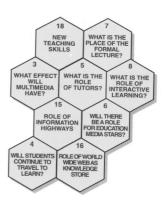

Step 4 - Naming Clusters

- The facilitator now guides the group to take each cluster in turn and tease out a title that expresses the unique meaning of that combination of factors in the situation.
- This helps to focus thinking and provides a valuable overview of the issues.
- It can be useful in a group situation to log suggested titles on a flipchart and then choose the title that attracts the most energy from the group.
- These titles represent the basis of the decision areas the group will be working with to generate options.

This is how our example group has titled their clusters:

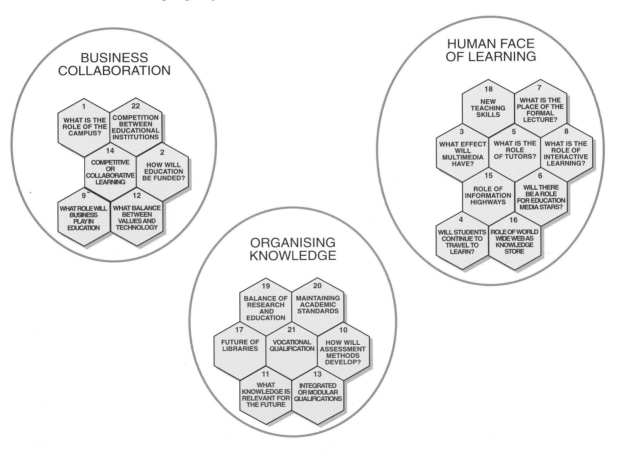

Step 5 - Formulating Decision Options

- Take each of the cluster titles and re-formulate it as a decision option or proposed action. This needs to be fairly specific and practical; your best shot at what you would like to make happen in the future. These options will be tested against the scenarios in the following section. This means that each decision option will be looked at in the light of a given possible future and adjusted for maximum effectiveness in that future.

- Where you have more than four clusters, choose three or four which seem to have the most potency. In our example we have chosen three.

If you look at the example offered by our educational group that follows, you will see how each cluster title has been converted into a specific actionable statement:

Three Areas of Decision Option

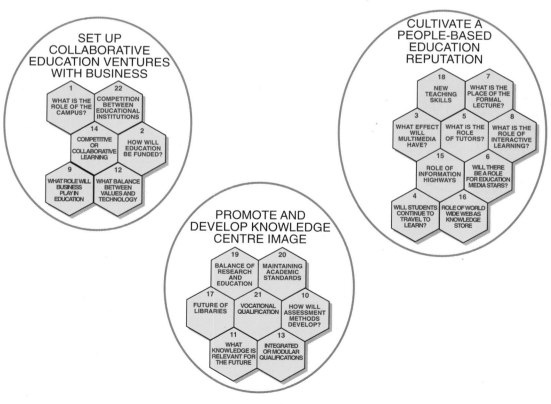

Using the Idon Decision/Scenario Matrix

In Chapter 6 we described in detail how a group of people can conceive of and create several rich and distinct scenarios in relation to a decision intent. Earlier in this publication we explored how the 'first causal heuristic' - our tendency to assume our easiest interpretation of a situation must be reality - affects judgement and in turn our understanding of what options are open to us. The process we have described so far gives us a way to enhance our understanding and enables us to identify and clarify a wider set of options as well as sharpening up our intent.

Having now established both the scenario 'worlds' and our decision options, we need a technique that both challenges us and helps us entertain how these options might manifest or turn out in each of the different future worlds.

There are several benefits from this. Since our expected future rarely comes about exactly as anticipated, this exercise gives us more preparedness for what we may otherwise experience as shocks, surprises and sudden turns of fortune.

Since unexpected challenges demand a sudden and altered approach, the exercise provides the opportunity of a simulation under controlled circumstances together with providing the luxury of time! As a result we gain space for creative planning, a chance to seek further information, advance opportunity to prepare for contingencies along with the ability to monitor trends. The advantages delivered for even minor improvements in shared thinking and development along these lines can offer a decisive competitive edge.

Purpose
The purpose of this technique is to provide a structure for conversation around the scenarios and to arrive at a set of statements which represent our decision options in each one. Whilst each statement will be terse, it will be packed with meaning for the participants. The basic exercise is to ask, "What if we pursued this course of action in that world?".

Preparations
This technique is best done on at least two metal-backed whiteboards, preferably in a supportive environment for group work.

You need
- a large metal-backed whiteboard (3' x 4' is a good size)
- a set of magnetic rectangles from the Idon Scenario Kit: 2 each of different colours to represent the scenarios, 3 or 4 red to represent the decision options, up to 16 yellow for the generative impact cells and 3 or 4 green for the robust options
- dry-wipe pens
- a duster
- a PC with Idons-For-Thinking™ software

	SCENARIO A	SCENARIO B	SCENARIO C	SCENARIO D	
DECISION OPTION 1	1A	1B	1C	1D	ROBUST OPTION 1
DECISION OPTION 2	2A	2B	2C	2D	ROBUST OPTION 2
DECISION OPTION 3	3A	3B	3C	3D	ROBUST OPTION 3
	COMPETENCE A	COMPETENCE B	COMPETENCE C	COMPETENCE D	

The Facilitation Steps

The key challenge to the facilitator is to stimulate *generative* or new thinking, as opposed to associative thinking, in the group. The generative power is in the imaginative playing out in the mind of the decision option in the context of a given scenario. This requires that the members of the group enter into each scenario/decision area fully, as if it were a reality, excluding all other considerations and then run a kind of mental simulation or rehearsal of how their decision would interact in that world. The main tool to structure that work is the *scenario matrix*.

This is a generative matrix where each cross-over cell represents the fundamental question, "What if we pursued this course of action in that world?" At the left side in red are the selected decision options (three are picked here in the example). At the top we place the scenario titles or "stories" (we have four from the previous exercise, picked out in violet, blue, brown and silver). The conclusions are drawn out horizontally (also violet, blue, brown and silver) and vertically (green).

Step 1 - Setting Up the Matrix
Although this can be done in advance (to get the spacing in line) it is important to take the group through the set-up to prepare people's minds.

- Brief people on the (three) decision options selected for priority attention down the left side.
- Brief people on the summary of each scenario which is arrayed across the top.
- Explain that each cell (yellow) where a generative impact falls is a "what if?" question we are going to investigate.

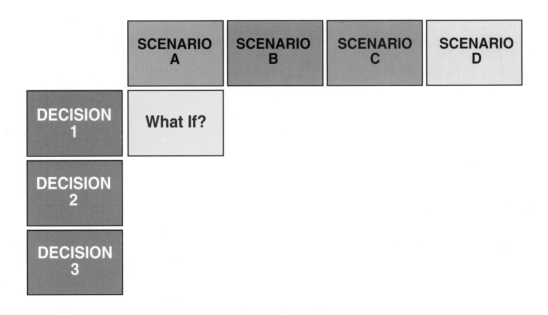

Step 2 - **Working Through a Scenario**

- Present the first scenario (A) by means of slides, story telling and discussion so that the group has brought it alive and can see how that world is plausible. Remember that this is as much an action of imagination as it is of memory and logic.
- Having established that world, take Decision Option 1 and ask the key question:

"What would be the consequences of pursuing Decision Option 1 in Scenario A?"

- Capture people's responses on flip charts.
- Summarise the gist of the conversation onto the yellow idon 1A.

In this example, our group has posed the question "What would be the consequences of pursuing Business Collaboration in the scenario "Catch as Catch Can?" and they have summarised their thoughts thus:

		SCENARIO A CATCH AS CATCH CAN	SCENARIO B JOIN TO LEARN	SCENARIO C CONVENIENT COMMUNITY	SCENARIO D BEING THERE	
DECISION OPTION 1	SET UP COLLABORATIVE EDUCATION VENTURES WITH BUSINESS	DIFFICULT UNLESS NICHED				
DECISION OPTION 2	PROMOTE AND DEVELOP KNOWLEDGE CENTRE IMAGE					
DECISION OPTION 3	CULTIVATE A PEOPLE-BASED EDUCATION REPUTATION					

- Repeat this process for Decision Options 2 and 3

The result our education group came up with follows:

	CATCH AS CATCH CAN	JOIN TO LEARN	CONVENIENT COMMUNITY	BEING THERE	
SET UP COLLABORATIVE EDUCATION VENTURES WITH BUSINESS	DIFFICULT UNLESS NICHED				
PROMOTE AND DEVELOP KNOWLEDGE CENTRE IMAGE	MUST BE GLOBALISED				
CULTIVATE A PEOPLE-BASED EDUCATION REPUTATION	NOT MUCH APPEAL				

Step 3 - Working Through The Other Futures
It is often a good idea to take a short break at this point so that the story of Scenario A can be dropped and the group can be ready to take up the story of Scenario B.
The process then continues:

- Present the second scenario (B) again using whatever slides, story telling and discussion you have available to bring the story alive.
- Work through each decision in that world as in Step 2.
- Take another short break and repeat with scenarios (C) and (D).
- You should end up with twelve conversations logged and twelve summaries on yellow idons as shown.

An example of a matrix completed to this stage by our educational group follows:

		SCENARIO A	**SCENARIO B**	**SCENARIO C**	**SCENARIO D**
		CATCH AS CATCH CAN	JOIN TO LEARN	CONVENIENT COMMUNITY	BEING THERE
DECISION OPTION 1	SET UP COLLABORATIVE EDUCATION VENTURES WITH BUSINESS	DIFFICULT UNLESS NICHED	HIGH APPEAL	FOR LOCAL EMPLOYMENT	ONLY WITH TOP RATING	
DECISION OPTION 2	PROMOTE AND DEVELOP KNOWLEDGE CENTRE IMAGE	MUST BE GLOBALISED	LINK TO VOCATIONS	NOT SO CRITICAL	CONCENTRATED CENTRES	
DECISION OPTION 3	CULTIVATE A PEOPLE-BASED EDUCATION REPUTATION	NOT MUCH APPEAL	APPRENTICE-SHIP STYLE	LOCAL PROMINENCE	STRONG APPEAL	

Step 4 - Extracting Robustness and Contingency

So far, the constant thread in each exercise has been to focus on a given scenario. In order to develop a sound guideline for action regardless of which future may emerge, we now need to consider each decision option in all the scenarios (the "what ifs") and find the best underlying option trend. We call this developing *robust options* for the future.

- Make sure everyone is clear about Decision Option 1.
- Carefully read across the summaries in the row next to it (idons 1A ,1B, 1C and 1D).
- Revisit the record of the individual session that led to that summary if the sense of the content is lost.
- Tease out any common threads across the row that suggest an option that would stand up in any future.
- Further refine this option by identifying any changes of action that would be specific to a given world (such as things to stop or different things to start). This is the contingent part of the option and prepares us for the improbable.
- Summarise these conclusions on the green idon at the end of the first row: the Robust Option 1 (details can be logged on a flip chart or in the "Notes" function of Idons-For-Thinking™ software).

- Repeat the above process for the other two Decision Options until you have three robust options logged.

In our example, the robust options chosen by our group came out like this:

	CATCH AS CATCH CAN	JOIN TO LEARN	CONVENIENT COMMUNITY	BEING THERE	
SET UP COLLABORATIVE EDUCATION VENTURES WITH BUSINESS	DIFFICULT UNLESS NICHED	HIGH APPEAL	FOR LOCAL EMPLOYMENT	ONLY WITH TOP RATING	ESTABLISH A HIGH-VALUE POSITION WITH LOCAL SUPPORT & ROLL-OUT POTENTIAL
PROMOTE AND DEVELOP KNOWLEDGE CENTRE IMAGE	MUST BE GLOBALISED	LINK TO VOCATIONS	NOT SO CRITICAL	CONCENTRATED CENTRES	ACCUMULATE KNOWLEDGE CONTENT WITH VOCATIONAL RELEVANCE & SEVERAL DISTRIBUTION OPTIONS
CULTIVATE A PEOPLE-BASED EDUCATION REPUTATION	NOT MUCH APPEAL	APPRENTICE-SHIP STYLE	LOCAL PROMINENCE	STRONG APPEAL	DEVELOP PEOPLE REPUTATION WITH OPTIONS TO PROMOTE THIS THROUGH MULTI-MEDIA

Step 5 - Identifying Core Competencies

The idea here is to look at the (three) vertical options for each of the scenarios and see what competencies you need to develop in order to implement these options successfully.

- Revisit briefly Scenario A.
- Read the three rectangles in that column: 1A, 2A and 3A.
- Develop ideas on what core competence would enable high performance in the given world.
- Summarise your thinking in the corresponding idon at the bottom of the row: Competence A.

	SCENARIO A	SCENARIO B	SCENARIO C	SCENARIO D	
DECISION OPTION 1	1A	1B	1C	1D	ROBUST OPTION 1
DECISION OPTION 2	2A	2B	2C	2D	ROBUST OPTION 2
DECISION OPTION 3	3A	3B	3C	3D	ROBUST OPTION 3
	COMPETENCE A	COMPETENCE B	COMPETENCE C	COMPETENCE D	

- Repeat for each of the other scenarios to complete the Idon Scenario Matrix.

This is the completed matrix as generated by our example group:

	CATCH AS CATCH CAN	JOIN TO LEARN	CONVENIENT COMMUNITY	BEING THERE	
SET UP COLLABORATIVE EDUCATION VENTURES WITH BUSINESS	DIFFICULT UNLESS NICHED	HIGH APPEAL	FOR LOCAL EMPLOYMENT	ONLY WITH TOP RATING	ESTABLISH A HIGH-VALUE POSITION WITH LOCAL SUPPORT & ROLL-OUT POTENTIAL
PROMOTE AND DEVELOP KNOWLEDGE CENTRE IMAGE	MUST BE GLOBALISED	LINK TO VOCATIONS	NOT SO CRITICAL	CONCENTRATED CENTRES	ACCUMULATE KNOWLEDGE CONTENT WITH VOCATIONAL RELEVANCE & SEVERAL DISTRIBUTION OPTIONS
CULTIVATE A PEOPLE-BASED EDUCATION REPUTATION	NOT MUCH APPEAL	APPRENTICE-SHIP STYLE	LOCAL PROMINENCE	STRONG APPEAL	DEVELOP PEOPLE REPUTATION WITH OPTIONS TO PROMOTE THIS THROUGH MULTI-MEDIA
	REMOTE TUTORING EXPERTISE	DEVELOP VOCATIONAL TRACK RECORD	INVOLVING LOCAL STAKEHOLDERS	BREAKTHROUGH FOR WORLD CLASS PERFORMANCE	

Drawing Conclusions From the Scenario Matrix

Getting the most out of the scenario matrix requires a clear understanding of how the summarisation across the rows (the Decision Options) and down the columns (Competencies) works. In this section the main kinds of outcome are described.

Firstly let us look at the horizontal dimension which reviews a particular strategy, policy or option in several scenarios. The aim is to discover what actions might sustain us through all scenarios and what actions we may need to be flexible about depending on which way the world turns out. There are four main types of conclusion that might be drawn, although it may not happen that all four crop up in any given exercise.

- *actions we should be doing anyway but we overlooked*
  Asking "what if?" in any scenario can stimulate us to see other options or modifications to decisions that had not previously occurred to us. If we find one that is valid in all scenarios and is of benefit, then we have found a clear practical action that we need to be taking. Some people call these "no brainers" in that once the point has been seen the decision is virtually automatic. However, this can also include powerful actions that increase our resilience; that is, our ability to be flexibly successful in any future.

- *actions we should take until unfolding events show we could drop them*
  We may find that to survive and thrive in one of our scenarios there is a specific action that is needed, but only in that scenario. Since, by definition from our original uncertainties, we do not know which future is going to unfold, we need to take some action and make some investment in it. However, we also monitor the environment carefully in that area and if there is strong indication that a particular scenario is <u>not</u> going to happen, then we are ready to drop it. This is a kind of strategic contingency planning but one where we cannot put off investment. There is a risk premium to pay.

- *actions we need to have ready for a specific future*
  This is somewhat similar to the previous one except that it tends to be a mental rehearsal of "what to do if", like an alternative plan. As such it is more like a conventional strategic plan.

- *actions to influence the future positively or negatively*
  Where we see that a particular scenario is favourable to us compared to others, we may be able to take action in areas that tend to push events in the direction of that scenario. This may sound

like an option just for big institutions like governments. But in modern business, for example, recent history shows that very small entrepreneurs can take action to shape a future in their favour on an almost unimaginable scale.

Secondly, let us look at the vertical dimension. Here we are dealing with a single scenario and looking at the distinctive competencies we would need to be successful in that future world. The development of core competence is not something which can be carried out quickly and so in a fast changing and uncertain world, this is a big challenge.

- *robust core competencies essential for all futures*
  Having characterised what we need to be good at to win or be successful in each scenario, we may notice that there is something we need to be good at in <u>all</u> possible future worlds. If it is something we are currently poor at or even lack altogether, then we get a strong message about taking action in this area.

- *directional distinctive capabilities to give advantage in the longer term future*
  Remember that, by definition, no scenario is itself a prediction. We may be drawn to place bets on a given scenario but that is not itself part of multi-future thinking where all are treated as equally plausible. However, our scenario work may reveal a general trend or even a paradigm change which has a ring of inevitability about it, even though we cannot see its precise form. In that case we may find that we need to set a direction of organisational development or even transformation that will prepare us for that kind of future.

- *contingent core competencies to win a particular future*
  We may find that one of our futures is so different from our current world that we would be unlikely to do well in that world. Although we cannot predict it will happen, equally, we cannot predict that it will not. In which case we may need to risk resources to develop that special competence to be sure that, if things do go that way, we will be ready and able to take up the challenge as an opportunity.

- *lateral leap competencies we need but have no basis for at present*
  Sometimes, the scenario exercise can have a powerful effect on our creative thinking and insight. We see possibilities for new worlds that we have not entertained before. Perhaps something that the experts say is twenty years away might happen in just three or four. Perhaps we could contribute to making it happen and command a large piece of the action. This is a lateral leap, however, because such a step of development is unlikely to link closely to anything we are doing now.

To sum up these main points:

Typical Conclusions from the Scenario Matrix

HOW RESILIENT ?	HOW COMPETENT ?
• actions we should be doing anyway but we overlooked	• robust core competencies essential for all futures
• actions we should take until unfolding events show we should drop them	• directional distinctive capabilities to give advantage in the longer term future
• actions we need to have ready for a specific future	• contingent core compentencies to win in a specific future
• actions to influence the future positively or negatively	• lateral leap competencies we need but have no basis for at present

THE JOURNEY THROUGH SCENARIO THINKING

Having surveyed the whole process it will be useful to recap the whole picture in a slightly different way. The diagram on the next page summarises the essential steps of thinking that the method has taken us through. Each step is a different perceptual and intellectual task, and each step has its own "feel" or energy. This feel is essential for good facilitation and helps the flow of work for both experienced and inexperienced people.

1. *Strategic Need*
   A policy or strategic direction is formulated.
2. *Environmental Factors*
   From this, a set of potentially significant environmental factors is identified.
3. *Pivotal Uncertainties*
   From these factors, pivotal uncertainties are identified.
4. *Sub-Plot Clusters*
   "Connected-ness" is revealed among these uncertainties which are grouped into clusters which then represent a major uncertainty or "sub-plot".
5. *Set of Scenarios*
   From the interplay of these sub-plots, scenarios are created which embody the uncertainties as stories of the future.
6. *Decision Issues*
   Meanwhile, decision issues are surfaced around the policy direction.

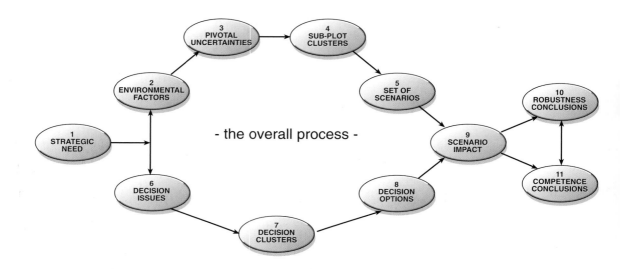

- the overall process -

7.   *Decision Clusters*
      These decision issues form clusters which indicate areas of choice.
8.   *Decision Options*
      These decision areas are reframed as decision options - a form which can be tested in the "what if?" of each scenario.
9.   *Scenario Impact*
      Each decision option is tried out in each scenario creating a series of "mental rehearsals" which can both evaluate and stimulate new thinking.
10.   *Robustness Conclusions*
      Conclusions are drawn about the robustness or resilience of the intended decision options.
11.   *Competence Conclusions*
      Conclusions are also drawn about the distinctive competence needed for success in a given scenario.

So what do you actually do or decide?

The interesting point here is to recognise that, since this method for scenario thinking is not a forecasting or predictive one, most of the uncertainties at the beginning still stand. The important thing is that now they have become crystal clear whereas before they existed as buried assumptions or worries. So final decision outcomes then fold back to be made in the light of the re-tuned intuitions, preferences and perceived risks for the next step that has to be taken.

In that sense decision-making is a learning journey into the unknown. The essential value of having done scenario thinking is that both distance and peripheral vision have been enhanced, more is taken into account, and the present situation is seen in a whole new light within the shared mental models of the participants.

Over time and as action proceeds, more factors will emerge and at some point a whole new reframe of scenarios will be needed to test the future from the new "present".

Scanning the Present for the Future - Cognitive Priming

Another benefit of this process is related to what psychologists call *cognitive priming*. This is the principle, demonstrated by many experiments, that we do not see things or pick up information about things unless first we have entertained the idea that such signals from the environment exist. Without a mental vision that something *could be*, we will miss the signals (often weak) that tell us it *will be*.

The exercise on pages 88 - 91 of searching for evidence of the future in the present is an illustration of this. People going through this exercise often report that they start with the view that some event in a scenario could not possibly happen, then they reach a point where it might be possible, but not for a long time to come. Then they report having noticed something in today's newspaper that it is happening now!

So another use you can make of the scenarios is to use them as search templates for exploring the environment and checking for indicators of development so that you get early warning. Whether your aim is competitive advantage or policy integrity, the extra lead time this can give (learning faster than the competition or anticipating changing circumstances) can make all the difference between success and failure.

PRACTISING MULTI-FUTURE THINKING

- for the best results, persevere once through the whole process to where you extract the conclusions from the scenario matrix because the point of some of the earlier stages becomes clearer as you see how they build up and are used

- however, you can also try each module separately and find that you get a clarification of that stage

- the kind of result you get will depend on a combination of your strategic thinking skills, your facilitation skills and the ease with which you pick up the visual methods

- there is greater in-depth psychology behind the methods than may at first be apparent and this will naturally boost confidence in practice

- training in the methods can greatly accelerate achieving the benefits

- complex high-level projects are best tackled with an experienced coach/ facilitator

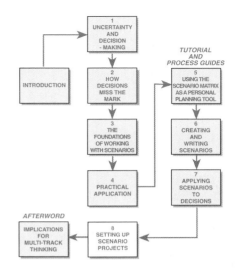

Chapter Eight

SETTING UP SCENARIO PROJECTS

- **Balancing Depth and Ownership**
  - **Methods For Gaining Depth**
- **Methods for Gaining Ownership**
- **Linking Scenario Work to Management Practice**

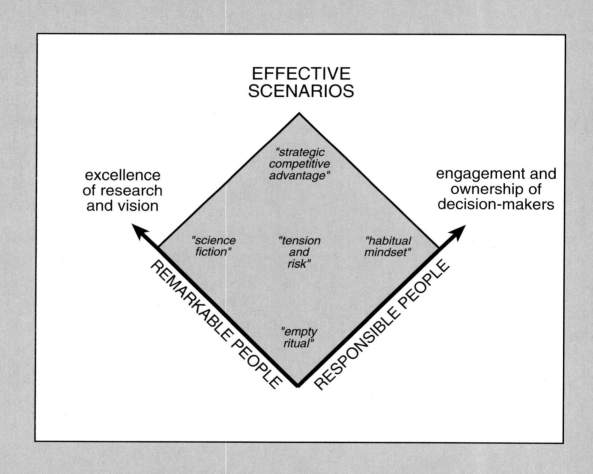

CHAPTER EIGHT

SETTING UP SCENARIO PROJECTS

There are many ways to carry out scenario projects depending on the aims, the resources and the skills of those involved in the process. At the individual or personal end of the spectrum, just an hour of multi-future thinking can radically improve the way we deal with our own uncertainties and ambiguities.

At the other end of the spectrum a major exercise may take several months, a team of people and a sizeable budget.

The important guiding principle is to balance depth and ownership. This dilemma is more fundamental than the resources because it relates directly to the effectiveness of the scenarios.

Balancing Depth and Ownership

By depth we mean the quality of investigation, research and thinking that goes into the content of the scenarios. Given that one aim of scenario thinking is to challenge us to "think outside the box" of our usual mindset, it is helpful to draw on views of the future which are not congruent with and even directly contradict our usual view. It is also important that, where appropriate, there is some rigorous investigation to serve as a basis for the scenario ingredients. On the diagram this is labelled "excellence of research and vision" and is on the axis called "remarkable people".

By ownership we mean the extent to which the decision-makers, those who hold the power to act, have internalised the scenarios and are truly engaged in multi-future thinking. All too often the decision-makers will reject scenarios (especially awkward ones) developed by other people and so nullify the impact. This leaves them stuck in their old mindset. On the diagram this is labelled "engagement and ownership of decision-makers" and is on the axis called "responsible people".

The challenge is to ensure we have a balanced involvement in both axes. If we just go for quality research then scenarios will be viewed as science fiction by the decision-makers. If we just go for executive participation we may end up re-inforcing a dangerous perspective that is never challenged. Avoiding both will be simply an empty ritual.

117

What often happens is that the two requirements are in conflict with each other. The researchers or planners want to increase executive involvement but are not given the time or money to make this possible. On the other hand the executives want to increase their feeling of control and so create taboo areas that never get looked into.

The facilitator has to guide the group through this tension zone to reach the point where scenario thinking really can give competitive advantage or genuine new insight. This has to be worked at in a flexible way. There is no easy formula.

Methods for Gaining Depth

Good scenarios require the input of a wide variety of perspectives which should reach way beyond the mindset of the individual subject or the organisation. Some companies have set up "visioning networks" populated by people from very different disciplines and not necessarily sharing the values of the client. Others create a map of stakeholders and relevant areas at the beginning of the project and find representative people from each area.

In both cases interviews are carried out to elicit the views of the future held by each person. Non-directive interview techniques are best*. The output of the interviews is correlated and creates a kind of "lego kit" of raw material for scenario building.

Even if the resources are not available for extensive networking, the open interview method can help access the peripheral vision (of people) which often intuitively goes beyond the official mindset and releases some of the necessary challenges.

This is the axis of *remarkable people*.

Methods for Gaining Ownership

Multi-future thinking has real impact only when it takes place in the mind of the decision-makers which means that they have to internalise the scenarios.

---

* Idon can offer training in "open cognitive mapping" interview techniques which enable this kind of work to be done with both depth and reliability.

The most powerful way to achieve this is to involve the decision-makers in the scenario creation process. This initially seems time-consuming but two factors compensate for this. With good facilitation and methods, such as those outlined in this handbook, the time this takes is quite short: perhaps an interview and a couple of days at a workshop. Also, once involved in the process, most executives report great personal benefit from the stretch to their thinking that the process requires and so are gaining benefit before reaching the climax of the scenario matrix.

Where this is not possible there are some part-way approaches which help. In a management team, for example, there may be one executive who can devote the time and so help develop ownership on the, "I was there and saw that; you'd better believe it!" principle. Another way is to take the sketch scenarios and involve the executive team in a brief time-line exercise to experience a taste of imaginative creation within each scenario.

Failing this, the minimum requirement is some preliminary warm-up discussions, an excellent and lively presentation and an after-dinner discussion on the meaning and plausibility of the scenarios before running a scenario matrix workshop.

This is the *responsible people* axis.

Linking Scenario Work to Management Practice

A scenario exercise can all too easily become a "one-off" or something repeated every couple of years. This can be helpful but it is not the development of multi-future thinking capability. For this, scenario thinking has to become a way of life, a recurring thread in the strategic conversation of the organisation.

The most effective way of linking scenarios of the future to day-to-day work is through sharing the task of environmental scanning. Any scenarios, however long-range they might be, have their roots in perception of the present; there are always pockets of the future in the present. This is easy to see in science and technology, where today's laboratory experiment may be tomorrow's household commodity.

Everyone involved should be charged with taking the scenarios and searching their current environment (newspapers, magazines, reports, conversations and conferences) for clues that fit or contrast the scenarios. A personal portfolio should be built up and, say, every three months, shared and reviewed. It is helpful to set up scenario rooms for this where clippings can be posted and groups can meet to review current decisions or plans in the light of what is emerging.

This process depends on "cognitive priming", a term psychologists use to describe an essential principle of how the brain picks up information from the environment. If your mind has not entertained the thought, you will not pick up the information that tells you it is happening. This is often called being "blind sided". Putting a twist on the old saying, "what the eye don't see, the heart won't grieve over", we can say instead, "what the mind don't entertain you will miss and come to grief over".

Such "weak signals", as some planners call them, then become part of the organisation's awareness and alertness to its changing environment. This in turn can inform the decision-makers and allow them to judge when a given set of scenarios is getting stale, thus signalling that it is time for a new round.

"The Future Usually Holds More Than We Expect"

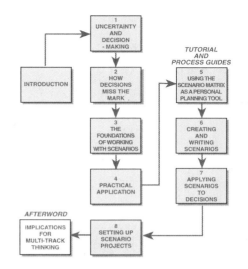

AFTERWORD

Implications For Multi-Track Thinking
Scenarios of the Future - Scenarios of the Past - Scenarios of the Present

- **Gambling with Commitment**
- **Scenarios of the Present, Scenarios of the Past**
- **Four Ways We Neglect Present Reality**
- **The Healthy Intellect**
- **Intuition: Valid Impressions of the Future**
- **Healthy Faculties of Intuition and Creativity**

AFTERWORD

Implications For Multi-Track Thinking:
Scenarios of the Future - Scenarios of the Past - Scenarios of the Present

"And the end of our exploration will be
to arrive where we started
and know the place for the first time."

T.S. Eliot 'The Four Quartets'

Our desire for certainty and predictability has systemic implications. How we see things can affect events on many levels. When we make the step to seeing several equally plausible futures, we begin to change the way we see the world and hence our choices are different. We are part of the equation that makes the future.

Experienced practitioners such as Arie de Geus* and Kees Van der Heijden* have made invaluable contributions to understanding how all this relates to decision-making. The practical methods in this book provide a way to facilitate the experience of seeing the future differently, both personally and in teams.

Behind these methods lies a deeper insight that multiple-track thinking is important, not just in relation to the future, but in relation to the past, as well as to the present. By multiple-track thinking we mean the capability to entertain more than one viewpoint of "reality", treating each as equally plausible. By *practising* thinking in multiple 'worlds', individually and collectively, we activate a cognitive capability far more significant and robust in the long term than a mechanism for 'best prediction'. Over time, with direct engagement, practitioners undergo a permanent change, acquiring a mental agility and insight beyond "thinking in a box" that enables a better understanding of how underlying forces can impact on and affect each other. The foundation for this is knowing the basis on which we build our understanding and opinion - the process that authenticates viewpoints and decides which direction we should be looking in.

On what do we build our opinions of the future and base our way forward? Even if 'facts' appear to be constant, straight-forward and highly predictable and we have not fallen into the

* see Bibliography

trap of assuming logical consistency, there remains the question: are external factors all we need to take into account? *Our individual and collective interpretations* of *the past and the present,* including personal interest, also affect what actually happens. We are deeply implicated in the scenarios in which we decide to act out our future.

In order to understand the future better, we need to explore more closely the different opinions, intentions, inconsistencies and underlying assumptions going into our interpretation of the *present* and their basis. Multiple-track thinking is not only necessary when looking at the future but also when examining the present, and for reviewing the past from a wider horizon, with greater perspectives. In turn, a cognitive capability of insight and flexibility can be developed, not just toward scenarios of the future but multi-track investigation of the present, as well as multi-track interpretation of the past!

These ideas are important for personal and organisational learning as well as for sound strategic thinking. Using practical techniques to model these issues prior to scenario planning provides a more thorough and robust coverage of multi-future thinking, whilst again confirming scenario thinking as an invaluable tool for organisational learning.

Gambling with Commitment

Any form of prediction is a gamble, since in a predictive state we can never be absolutely certain of the outcome. When trapped in a first causal heuristic, we tend to believe in the future we can most easily imagine. As a result we will invest most heavily in the future we have most faith in coming about - the *First Causal Scenario Heuristic,* and consequently that is where the heaviest commitment is placed.

We can check this is true by taking a reading on what we invest in, as the demands of investment betray where our deepest confidence lies! We may hold all kinds of ideas and intentions but what we actually *do,* where we *actually* place our resources, betrays our real alignment. In this light we are looking at prediction as investment and our decision-making as most challenging and emotionally engaging wherever we have a high degree of personal investment at stake. We have a choice then, as to whether or not to challenge the first causal scenario heuristic - whether to open 'Pandora's Box'. Understanding and exposing the true disposition of a group of people is important where stakes are high, as any hidden or suppressed driving force will influence the result.

Surprisingly, in practice, the registering of a multiple future most often does not cause fear or anxiety but quite the contrary: it tends to dissolve them. Exposing the uncertainties permits them to be consciously and creatively explored, thus enabling the decision-makers to create a competitive edge through the generation of more options.

Scenarios of the Present, Scenarios of the Past

As the validity of scenario-building is based on the validity of the reality model used to construct the scenarios, it is important that this model is current, explicit and not an old interpretation carried through from the past. Often our scenarios *are* overly contaminated by the past, and the way to avoid this is to look closely at our current understandings of the past and put *them* through a "what if" test also - questioning assumptions and building multi-track thinking of the *present*.

Taking into account alternative interpretations of the current state, we can track back into the stories we tell ourselves about our past and see them afresh. We can examine the construction of these stories, the assumptions we have made and the implications of our approach.

This is a process we sometimes do naturally when enough time has passed following an important event. Distanced from the event to where it feels safe to revisit it, we can review and liberate ourselves from the trap of restrictive interpretations and recurring cycles. By deliberately exercising multi-track thinking of the past - alternative history modelling - we can greatly assist the re-framing process that in turn gives us the opportunity of destiny control. By refreshing our understanding of the past we redefine our relationship with the present.

If our interpretation of the present does not closely resemble what is actually happening, this will compromise our attempts at multi-future thinking. Without multi-track understanding of the present we may not have chosen the right areas to look at when developing multi-track thinking towards the future. The real future is intimately connected with the real present and our interpretation of this present must be acute.

Greater consciousness and understanding of the present will inevitably deliver greater flexibility in the design of its systems. So long as we are betting on single dimensional thinking we are gambling a great deal more than we need to, taking unnecessary risks and preparing the way for shock when beliefs are shattered by an emergent reality.

Four Ways We Neglect Present Reality

There are four ways in which we neglect the present reality by failing to question or investigate it. These are also the four ways in which people or institutions become dysfunctional in their behaviour or actions:

1) *Anxious Future*

   If we observe this state carefully in ourselves or others, we will see that whilst in it, the brain is trapped in a negative future fixation accompanied by all the fearful images that we generally conjure up to make it real. These negative projections of the future then entrap us in a form of time bondage - where time is the memory of the projected future. Studies show that as the brain projects these negative 'horror' images it is matched by a physical reaction - blood thrusting to the front of the brain. In this state it becomes even harder to question assumptions about this future and instead we generally invest more heavily in indulging the negativity. Unaware of the actual current reality and its alternative parallel potential trends, or 'random' occurrences, the victim(s) self-inflict a dysfunctional state.

2) *Fantasy Future*

   In this state one is experiencing a manic excitement towards the future - perhaps with expectations that one's 'ship will come in' and save one from the present predicament, or of a new partner, money.... This state provides the function of a great mental escape-hatch fully equipped with delusions of grandeur. Here the mind is trapped, held hostage by imagined future fulfilment of a positive and exciting kind. Here we are kept dysfunctional through mania: a positive-track future-fixation that destroys sanity or adequacy in the present. This is an extreme form of day-dreaming.

3) *The Negative Past*

   Here consciousness is trapped in the depressing and bitter past of missed opportunities, regret, burdens of guilt and anguish: one did not become what one hoped to in a previous fantasy; one is returning to the past to indulge in regret; remembering an old girlfriend or boyfriend; the regret that someone died and they were never told how much you cared. In this state the only future that could be accepted as 'real' would be if the past were undone.

4) *Positive past*

   Here living in the past is full of reminiscences of the 'golden old days' - dwelling on better times passed when 'the company was doing so well;' there was 'not so much crime';

'people were kind'; 'bread cost only...'. This is the state of home-sickness, nostalgia and longing to return to the 'good old past'. The only positive state possible in this condition is sadness toward the past. People in this condition tend to think conservatively and work for historic revival.

People living in the past are living more from conditioning and habit. They could be seen as "driving in their rear view mirror" and generally consider that what lies ahead should be firmly based on the past. These people usually do not look around until after they have crashed - if they recover - and are dangerous as decision-makers.

The time-bound brain of fantasy is slippery, being anywhere but in the present! Excitement, hype and illusion make its assessments and judgements unreliable. Over-enthusiasm towards the future is insubstantial and when the time-bound person is challenged they become tense, clumsy, get angry and blow up. In a state of unhappy chaos, everything takes a long time because of the anger and frustration.

The healthy brain state functioning in the present will tend toward perceiving everything as timeless and expansive. It will be more aware, alert, competent, flexible, effective, gracefully efficient and present, with a tendency towards multi-track thinking.

Clarity and inner stability are necessary for turning to the past or imagining a future that has value, but when these things are unbalanced and severely conflict with a greater reality model we must question them carefully. These four are all common states that we can generally observe without much difficulty. The decisive factor is both the degree of fixation as well as the capacity for flexibility and change.

The Healthy Intellect

The intellect of a human being or group of human beings then, has a double capability to be developed:

A) *The Passive Side*
   in order to expand our awareness, we need to:

- develop multi-reality awareness of the present
- review those multiple presents through the study of multiple pasts

- visualise plausible multiple futures or scenarios

 All of these together then form a multi-track *judgement* of what is, what was and what could be.

B) *The Active Side*
in order to make valid plans for success in the future, we need to:

- be able to cross plans or options across many futures
- be much more flexible and alert to the signals of emergent situations
- be alert to and register changes in the environment

When we cross the road or drive a car we are using some degree of multi-track thinking in order to survive. If we use the example of crossing a street we can see how dangerous single-track thinking can be. A fictitious character, 'Brian', exercising multi-track thinking when crossing the street, will in addition to crossing safely (he is paying attention, his judgement is good, he is aware of sudden changes) do so more efficiently because he is also alert and open to seizing opportunities. Another fictitious character, 'Edward', upset over a quarrel with his wife, being emotionally disturbed, may fail to give necessary attention to possible dangers, assumes a clear crossing and gets hit by an on-coming vehicle!

If a flexible brain state is decisive for such a routine activity as crossing the street, surely we would not expect less of ourselves in other areas of our personal and work life? It would also follow that companies would want employees to be consciously working with this higher awareness and have concern as to what could be done to get this. A time-bound brain is neither optimal for its owner nor its employer! Scenario planning should be so thoroughly absorbed that all decision makers do it instinctively on every decision, not just in a workshop context. Applying multiple scenario thinking will affect the real quality of awareness, planning, actions and the ability to register appropriate information.

Without this cognitive tune-up, it is unlikely that creating scenarios alone will get the job done in the long term. Working with multi-track thinking should be thorough and change the state of decision-makers. If it is going to work it must become natural. In this view, scenario thinking is never a one-off exercise.

How many people develop the capability to suspend opinions and judgements in favour of exploring reality more widely and questioning assumptions? Probably not a high percentage.

However, a requisite degree of this needs to happen for organisational learning to be alive and well.

All decision-makers must count the cost of time-bound thinking and time-bound activity and consider its consequences:

* awareness becomes a fantasy, not a fact
* the time-bound mind projects awareness only as an ideal future state, not as an operational necessity.

Intuition: Valid Impressions of the Future

There is a form of prediction that is not gambling: this is "intuition". This faculty is potentially present in the cognitive system that is not time-bound. If the human brain is in a good state, open and responsive, it can actually receive valid impressions of future outcomes called intuitions.

Intuition has nothing to do with folk belief or belief fixations, although some scientists do interpret it in this way. Intuition is not superstition but a higher faculty. Roy Rowan, in 'The Intuitive Manager', pointed out that some successful managers and entrepreneurs have intuitions that allow them to adjust to the future better than managers who do not have this faculty. Only a system that has healthy multi-track thinking taking place has good intuition.

Passive Higher Functioning
Intuition is not an anxious state but requires quiet, steady observance. Should this faculty grow, watchfulness and restraint ensures protection against turning this also into a fixated belief system. Pursue the intuitive course - gamble - cautiously and watch for a good result. Study outcomes. Increasingly trust intuition as you verify it, along with its growth and effectiveness, but never lose touch with multi-track thinking. This is the passive (or judgement) side of higher functioning in the human brain.

Active Higher Functioning
If your action is effective and versatile you can begin to ignite natural creative power - creativity - in the form of the ability to plan the future, not just as an experience but as a decision-maker able to shape it. A decision-maker can make things happen in a way that would not have been possible had they not been arrived at consciously.

Healthy Faculties of Intuition and Creativity
"creativity favours the prepared mind"

In this way intuition and creativity can become available to multi-track thinkers and decision-makers. These faculties will not be analytical and concrete explanations cannot be made up about them. On the other hand, they will not be imaginary, nor will they be disconnected from living activity. There will be none of the invented aberrations we see from those who are caught in R&D cycles that have no connection with events and people. There will be no imitation of creation manifested as inappropriate inventiveness.

When companies buy into creativity they generally do so as an addition to their already-noisy brains, so that what is actually being bought is a form of self-deception that is not really creativity but a form of pretending. Intuition and creation happen more easily when one is free of the time-bound condition. A quiet, aware system can develop a higher order function - where being an aware entrepreneur is one definition of a genius.

Multi-track thinking can be a tremendous organisational learning and development tool to help get brains out of their time-bound condition. By modelling the past, the present and the future as multiple realities, we open up the potential for deeper insights to inform our choices. This may seem initially to be introducing unnecessary complexity, and would be so if we stopped here.

Beyond the complexity is the simple next step that avoids deviation, survives the unexpected and fulfils the vision. As a Supreme Court Judge said, "I fear simple decisions before complexity; after complexity a simple decision can be wise."

Bibliography

The Art of the Long View, Peter Schwartz, *Century Business (1991)*

Confident Decision Making, J. Edward Russo & Paul J.H. Schoemaker, *Guild Publishing (1989)*

Developing Strategic Thought, Bob Garrett (ed), *McGraw-Hill (1989)*

The Fifth Discipline Fieldbook, Peter M. Senge, Art Kleiner, Charlotte Roberts, Richard B. Ross & Bryan J. Smith, *Doubleday (1994)*

The Intuitive Manager, Roy Rowan, *Wildwood House (1987)*

The Living Company, Arie de Geus, *Harvard Business Press (1997)*

Planning as Learning, Arie de Geus, *extract from Harvard Business Review (1988)*

Scenarios: The Art of Strategic Conversation, Kees Van Der Heijden, *John Wiley and Sons (1997)*

Scenario Planning, Gill Ringland, *John Wiley (Autumn 1997)*

Thinking With Hexagons, Idon, *Idon Ltd (1996)*

GLOSSARY

There follows a glossary of terms used with special meaning in this Book.

active listening
the skill of taking in what someone is saying and confirming with them directly that you have understood what they have said and have not embellished it in any way.

annotating
adding text which elaborates the meaning of a summary statement made on flip chart or hexagon during visual facilitation

big flip-flops
a term used to describe how a group or cluster of uncertainties about the future might all resolve in one direction ("a big flip") or another ("a big flop")
(see also flip-flops and sub-plots)

blocking dynamics
the tendency of a team to establish group norms which become more important to uphold than new thinking or learning

brainstorming
a technique of opening up new thinking which requires an explicit rule of no criticism and an encouragement to keep a flow of ideas moving through association

capturer
the role in a facilitation session of writing down all the key points made by the working team in a way that will be or is accessible to the group, optimally using the Idons-For-Thinking software specially designed for this purpose (see also computer support facilitator)

capturing
the skill of faithfully recording contributions of team members (see also active listening)

capturing patterns
the skill of not only capturing points, but interrelationships of points represented graphically

catalyst
this can be a facilitator whose role is to add value by activating and stimulating a process without taking the decision power or a non-team member who contributes to the performance effectiveness of a team

causal loop diagrams
a technique of representing interaction between components of a system with feedback loops

changing the frame
stimulating a team to shift its mental perspective on a decision or problem

clustering
taking individual ideas or factors and placing them in interconnected groups avoiding simple classification so as to encourage the uncovering of different perspectives; at best, can be a form of generative thinking (usually done with magnetic hexagons)

cognitive mapping
a technique for eliciting people's mental models of a situation and enabling them to consolidate a team model (see also hexagon mapping & idonic modelling techniques)

cognitive priming
the deliberate research into ideas and information outside of our habitual perception of reality in order to take into account the principle that we do not see things or pick up information unless we have first entertained the idea that they might exist

combining
the power of the mind to take disconnected material and combine it into new useful patterns

common language
a shared understanding of reality which can be rapidly developed through visual facilitation techniques and which enables deeper communication in a culture empowering it to act as an organic whole

compression of a statement
the skill of taking a lengthy exposition of an idea and distiling it down without distortion into a succinct phrase for visibility in a group situation

computer support facilitator
person who takes a real time capture role during a facilitated session, often where the content is projected onto a screen and visible to participants, optimally using the Idons-For-Thinking software (see also capturer)

context shapers
factors that are common throughout a set of scenarios and are certain to shape the future environment with a relatively predictable impact

convergent
a process of thinking which takes a diverse set of information and narrows it down to a conclusion

core competence
a competence or skill identified as being needed by an organisation or person in any of the possible futures being tested in the Idon Scenario Matrix

decision intent
a general direction we intend to pursue in decision making (see also decision option)

decision issue
a shared focus of concern about future decision performance

decision option
a practical and specific intended future action choice formulated by a group to be tested against multiple possible futures in the Idon Scenario Matrix (see also decision intent and robust option)

decision power
the power and authority to implement or prevent decisions, particularly relevant where the ownership of the outcome of a process is truly shared by those with the power to act

design
the process of formulating an open-ended working process from a client brief

elicit
to draw information out of someone else's mind with his/her full co-operation

emergent process
a generative process in which a new form and content become manifest

energy level
the degree of attention, enthusiasm and mental sharpness that a group shows in working together

environment
the physical context in which facilitation is taking place, from the specific visual aids to the size and shape of the room

environmental scanning
the function of searching the current environment (e.g. world news, competitor behaviour, scientific developments) for clues that fit or contrast a set of scenarios (see also cognitive priming)

evaluating
a process of distillation of important and significant ideas from an original bank of divergent ideas

excursion
breaking away from usual trains of thought into something metaphorical or imaginative in order to stimulate new insights

expressing
giving external form to ideas or insights that normally remain submerged and unshared

facilitating
the art of helping a group through a process of shared thinking and conversation towards a common goal

facilitator
the person who plays the catalytic role of facilitating, usually a third party

feedback loop
an information pathway that modifies inputs or transformations as a result of output

first causal heuristic
the tendency to assume our habitual interpretation of a situation must be reality

flip-flops
a term used to simplify an uncertainty about the future as a resolution in one direction ("a flip") or another ("a flop")

framework
a skeletal discipline based on valid knowledge that helps people to evoke ideas and position them

functional integration
the integration through skilled facilitation of the knowledge of different functional experts in an organisation or group so as to broaden the vision and enrich the common language of that group

generating
creating new ideas or insights by the synthesis of already known factors

generative impact cells
the rectangles (usually coded yellow) in the main body of the Idon Scenario Matrix which represent the impact of the decision options in each of the scenario worlds and which generate new insights

generative thinking
the capacity of the mind to deal with unknown situations through creating and testing new hypotheses

genius
awareness free of the time-bound condition (see also time-bound brain)

hexagon mapping
a technique of recording and organising ideas on hexagonal tiles that can be put together and rearranged at will, taking advantage of the "left/right" brain functions and natural patterning ability of the brain (see also idon & idonic modelling techniques)

idon
a combination of an idea (in words) with an icon (in shape) - common example is the statement in a hexagon. This term is also used to denote the magnetic shapes in Idon kits

idonic modelling techniques
the action of creating visual models using magnetic idons on whiteboards or Idons-For-Thinking graphical software to rapidly surface and progress individual or group thinking (see also cognitive mapping)

idonic methods
an integrated range of visual techniques developed by Idon Research exemplified by the Idon Strategy Bridge

insight
an action in the mind of seeing a new factor or seeing from a new perspective - strong enough to impact on behaviour

interview
usually a 1:1 meeting in which information and viewpoints are elicited

intuitions
valid impressions of future outcomes

learning
the art of coming to knowing in the face of the unknown

mapping
the creation of a two-dimensional representation of an internal pattern of thought in order to make it visible and changeable

management team
a group of managers who are collectively responsible for some coherent business unit

mental alignment
the enhanced collective understanding achieved by a group using visual methods

mental models
the patterns of understanding in the brain that actually determine behaviour (deeper than what we may think we think)

mental simulation (rehearsal)
the visualisation in the mind of a facilitation sequence - in order to test its robustness and skill up for the real event

mindset
the dominant brain pattern in which all our thinking tends to get limited; breaking out of mindset is an important part of creative thinking

modelling
the action of creating visual and dynamic models to help a group become more aware of its assumptions

multi-future thinking
the deliberate development of the faculty of holding several equally plausible futures in mind (also known as scenario thinking)

multi-track thinking
the deliberate practice of thinking in multiple 'worlds' in order to better understand how underlying forces and impacts affect each other

natural agenda
the area of genuine but rather private concern in the minds of a group or team that can often take months to get to the formal agenda; deeper than plans and usually a source of emergent strategy; skilled facilitation can considerably reduce its time to surface thus creating competitive advantage

open-ended methods
methods where the outcome is unknown and the path is created as you walk it

ownership (of scenarios)
the extent to which the decision makers, those who hold the power to act, have internalised the scenarios and are truly engaged in multi-future thinking

pivotal uncertainties
uncertainties about the future whose outcome is uncertain and which may have strong directional consequences; areas that will determine the shape of different scenarios (see also uncertainties)

pockets of the future
evidence in the present of factors which indicate that an envisaged future is already happening now

potential jokers
unlikely high impact uncertainties about the future; factors to monitor on the 'corporate radar' in case they show signs of coming about (see also uncertainties)

process (in groups)
as distinguished from content - the way a group behaves and interacts as distinct from the subject it is talking about

robust option
a sound guide-line for action regardless of which future comes to pass; the best underlying option trend; summarised in the right-hand column of the Idon Scenario Matrix (see also decision option)

scenarios
contrasting stories of the future which stimulate "what if?" thinking beyond habitual limits

scenario matrix
a method developed by Idon for accelerating robust scenario thinking and decision making

scenario thinking
the deliberate development of multi-future thinking skills that improve how we are in the face of the unknown (see also multi-future thinking)

significant trends
uncertainties about the future which impact differently on distinct scenarios but whose effects can reasonably be anticipated

strategic management
an approach to strategic planning which leaves the ownership of generating the plan with the line executives not the planner

strategic modelling
the use of a variety of intellectual disciplines which add value to the strategic thinking of executives particularly in dealing with the question "what if?"

strategic intent
the focused intention to act of a group or corporation based on strategic conversation (see also 'decision intent')

strategic plan
a plan which aims to determine the longer term viability and success of an organisation

strategic thinking
the cognitive competence of creating strategy

sub-plots
these are titles generated using the Idon hexagon cluster "flip-flop" method and represent the two possible outcome states of a major uncertainty and are used as a basis for scenarios which embody the uncertainties as stories of the future
(see also flip-flops and big flip-flops)

suspension of judgement
the ability to put aside what is known about a subject and entertain other perspectives at least for an agreed period of time

task
the aim of a group that a facilitator is helping

team alignment
achieving congruence between the mental models of the team members

team-work
the conscious and skilled effort of all team members to achieve team effectiveness

thinking in a box
the tendency to remain in a 'one world' point of view or limited mindset where the most obvious perception of the world is seen to be the only valid one

time-bound brain
a brain that is not engaged in multi-track thinking and therefore less likely to be aware, alert, competent, flexible, effective and gracefully efficient (see also genius)

trigger question
a question designed to elicit responses from a group around a topic of current concern related to the thinking task

uncertainties
perceived ambiguous factors about the future which, when identified and clarified, provide the first step in scenario thinking and form the background of scenarios

vision
a mental image of a future set of conditions to be achieved

visual aids
specially designed visibility tools for enabling visual dialogue in groups

visual dialogue
the practice of enhanced intercommunication of ideas and generation of new insights through a combination of visual and verbal or written methods which make full use of the patterning ability of the human brain

visual feedback
the use of visual representation to help an individual or group become more aware of its thinking

visual thinking
a new art of dialogue that simultaneously combines visual and verbal forms of communication for the clarification and development of shared thought

weak signals
the signals from the environment, often very faint, which inform us that something we have entertained as a possibility may be actually happening now

workshop
a designed event in which on open-ended outcome is attempted through a designed team-work process

workshop output
the output of visual thinking in a text-graphical form; both a report and a contribution to an information database

APPENDIX

MAGNETIC KITS AND SOFTWARE TO SUPPORT SCENARIO THINKING

Group Scenario Kit

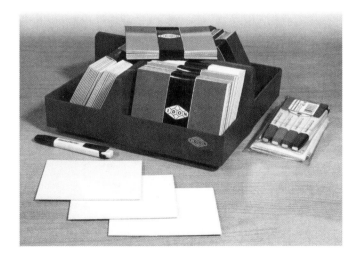

EACH KIT CONTAINS
- 88 Rectangles (5.5" x 5.5")
- Rotating Plastic tray
- Wallet of Drywipe Pens
- Duster
- Idon Scenario Thinking Book

Use this highly visible kit to share group scenario thinking. A magnetic whiteboard (available separately) of at least 4' x 3' is recommended.

Personal Scenario Kits

A2 Executive Scenario Kit

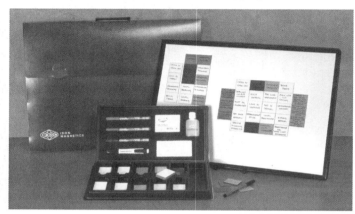

KIT CONTAINS:
Presentation Case containing

- 132 Rectangles (46 x 35mm)
- 3 Wetwipe Pens
- 1 Drywipe Pen
- Cleaning Sachets
- Water Bottle
- A2 Magnetics Liteboard® (594 x 420mm)
- A2 Black Portfolio Case
- Foldflat Easel
- Idon Scenario Thinking Book

Scenario Thinking Kit

KIT CONTAINS:
- 66 Rectangles (46 x 35mm)
- Miniboard (500 x 300mm)
- Silver Colour Case
- Wetwipe Pens
- Water Bottle, for cleaning
- Paper Tissues, for cleaning
- Idon Scenario Thinking Book

Use the above portable kits for personal and interpersonal scenarios. The Executive version provides ample modelling space with the double sided Liteboard®. The Scenario Thinking Kit is ideal for workshop or course members.

Hexagon Group Kit
(yellow)

EACH KIT CONTAINS
- 70 Hexagons 114mm (4.5")
- Rotating Plastic tray
- Wallet of Drywipe Pens
- Wallet of Wetwipe Pens
- Duster
- Hexagon Notepad
- User Manual,
  "Thinking With Hexagons"

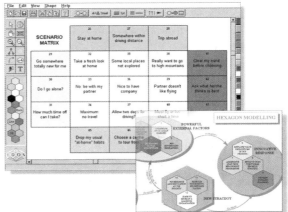

The Hexagon Group Kit is recommended for the preparatory stages of creating and writing scenarios. In addition magnetic Hexagons are ideal for collecting contributions and clustering ideas when formulating decision intent.

"Idons-For-Thinking" software

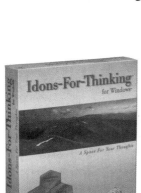

"Idons-For-Thinking" is a stand-alone creativity and decision support tool. In addition, the software is designed, along with the Magnetics Kits, to track group thinking in facilitated workshops. The software allows valuable discussion to be annotated in the models for feedback and future reference. It is particularly useful as a knowledge database of scenario thinking.

Win/Win95/NT versions available.

THE IDON GROUP

 The Idon Group is committed to supplying mutually supportive innovative services, tools and technologies for facilitating personal and organisational learning.

Idon Ltd
Research and Development

Idon Associates
Consulting and Facilitation

Idon Training
Training

Idon Magnetics
Visual Tools and Publications

Idon Software
Visual Thinking Software

 Idon Ltd provides the next generation products and services necessary for managing emergent new realities. Through well established developments in facilitating visual thinking and visual dialogue, Idon has a growing reputation for delivering deeper insight, better thinking and effective group dialogue essential for informed and coordinated action in new forms of organisation.

Idon Training offers personal and group training in graphical facilitation techniques and tools for applied visual thinking. Training in these methods include: rapid one-day induction courses; two and three-day workshops; modules across the Idon Facilitation Bridge; facilitator training and in-company Organisational Learning programmes.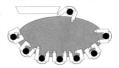

 **Idon Associates** provides services that help transform the decision thinking and learning capability in organisations. This is achieved through strategic consultancy and direct facilitation of management processes such as strategy review, scenario planning, accelerated project management and creative problem solving. Collaborative thinking methods innovated by Idon include hexagon mapping, concept mapping, scenario matrix, goal-oriented problem solving and flexible system modelling.

Idon Magnetics produces magnetic visual tools on whiteboards to support a wide range of group and personal thinking processes. The now famous hexagon technique was invented by Idon to supersede brainstorming and facilitates the rapid sharing of mental models in teams to evoke new thinking. Idon Magnetics also equips facilitation, training and learning environments.

 **Idon Software** supplies the original thinking software tool - now fully updated as Idons-For-Thinking - designed to support individuals as well as groups in the development, communication and tracking of the processes and contents of thinking. Training in using Idons-For-Thinking for capturing live facilitated group sessions is also offered.

For further information on Idon Services and Products, please contact Idon at:

Idon Ltd   Edradour House   Pitlochry   Perthshire   PH16 5JW   Scotland   UK
Tel: **(UK)   01796   473773**   Fax: **(UK)   01796   473880**   E-mail: **info@idongroup.com**
Or meet us on the Web at **http//www.idongroup.com**